2

*Thinking of...*

# Force.com as your key to the Cloud Kingdom?

*Ask the Smart Questions*

By Alok Misra & Ian Gotts

**Foreword by Parker Harris, cofounder, salesforce.com**

# Smart Questions™ Philosophy

*Smart Questions is built on 4 key pillars, which set it apart from other publishers:*

1. *Smart people want Smart Questions not Dumb Answers*
2. *Domain experts are often excluded from authorship, so we are making writing a book simple and painless*
3. *The community has a great deal to contribute to enhance the content*
4. *We donate a percentage of revenue to a charity voted for by the authors and community. It is great marketing, but it is also the right thing to do*

*www.Smart-Questions.com*

# Reviews

It's interesting that over the past 50 years, the software industry has not only gone through business cycles but also business model cycles. And even more interesting is that the critical issues in successful business models keep being forgotten, or assumed are being solved in the next newest iteration. What Gotts and Misra have done in their thinking here is to frame the problem well and clearly. Then by using the Q&A approach, they provide not only a great check list, but also a bite-sized chunks process to allow the reader to think about and understand the key issues at a engaged and detailed level. I'd recommend the book to any ISV or enterprise CIO thinking about what they might or could do in the Cloud space.

*Ken Horner, Principal, Deloitte*

*www.deloitte.com*

The Smart Questions approach makes the complicated simple. With its aptly labeled "Questions for Suits" and "Questions for Jeans", this is the book that an executive needs to read before making a go/no go decision about a Cloud Computing project. Author Alok Misra, who has helped us make that decision, lives and breathes this subject. He is an excellent guide.

*Michelle Nunn, CEO, Points of Light Institute*

*www.pointsoflight.org*

Thinking about building an app on Force.com? Well don't, at least not until you have read Alok and Ian's book. They'll guide you through the decisions you need to make to ensure you build a successful app, but more importantly lead you through the commercial questions you must address in order to make sure you can successfully monetize your development investment. Alok and Ian are well respected in the Force.com community and this book is a great place to start your journey with the Force.com platform.

*Jeremy Roche, CEO, FinancialForce.com & Chairman, CODA*

*www.financialforce.com*

This book, "Thinking of..." outlines the thinking and planning required to migrate a traditional software company to the "software as a service" model, using salesforce.com's Force.com platform. The book presents dozens of questions an ISV must ask itself before jumping into SaaS and many case study examples of companies that have failed and succeeded at their attempts to offer software as a service. It should serve as a useful guide to any company interested in making this shift.

**Penny Crosman, Executive Editor, Techweb**

*www.techweb.com*


Cloud computing has, of course, been around for decades – the challenge has always been how you make money on the stuff. Add Marc Benioff, Force.com, and stir, and a real Cloud ecosystem started wearing long pants in 2009. In the fall, Nucleus found Force.com developers could develop apps 4.9 times on Force.com than .NET or JAVA, and few believed they were "locked in" because they would be locked in with Microsoft or IBM using another language, and likely face a much longer time to market. But not everyone was successful in making their first million in the Cloud – largely because they hadn't worked out all the dumb stuff – such as their business model and development and support strategy. In Smart Questions, Alok and Ian lay out the key business and technical factors that developers enamored with (or puzzled by) Force.com should consider before they hit the sandbox. They highlight some of the inherent challenges traditional vendors face in adopting a Cloud strategy, both technical and financial. This is a good quick sanity check for new or existing companies considering a venture into the Cloud. The book highlights a lot of the business opportunities and realities facing salesforce.com partners today, and aspiring developers should take heed.

**Rebecca Wetteman, Vice President, Nucleus Research**

*www.nucleusresearch.com*

We started Salesforce.com and the Salesforce Foundation simultaneously as a new model for business. Make philanthropy a core part of the culture of the company and great things will happen. The 1-1-1 model (1 percent time; 1 percent equity; 1 percent product) has been helping nonprofits and making a difference from the very beginning. Force.com allows nonprofits to innovate in an unprecedented way. Not only have we seen them be able to become more efficient, but their innovation in areas such as social networking and campaign management is being adopted now by businesses too. Nonprofits such as Girls Inc and Points Of Light Institute have actually helped create commercial products such as volunteer and constituent management for nonprofits, that businesses are also interested in deploying. Who knew that ISV products would be coming from nonprofits? Navatar Group has been very successful in using Force.com to bring out the "entrepreneurial side" of nonprofits. Alok and Ian show us the path to bringing out the best in nonprofit innovation and entrepreneurial spirit, in this book. I strongly recommend this book to any nonprofit that seeks to save money and innovate in the Cloud.

**Suzanne DiBianca, Executive Director, Salesforce.com Foundation**

*www.salesforcefoundation.org*


We all have questions about Force.com, but Alok and Ian have answers, solid answers, answers to questions that I hadn't even thought of. Force.com can work well as a Cloud Computing platform, but only if you take into account all the issues that they cover with clarity and brevity.

**David Dobrin, President, B2B Analysts**

*www.b2banalysts.com*

It is tempting to dismiss Cloud Computing as another product of the well-oiled technology hype machine. However, Cloud reality is catching the hype as early adopters of the technology have demonstrated compelling business benefits include higher ROI and lowered TCO. Independent Software Vendors (ISV's) and Enterprise IT groups have many burning questions around if, how, and when they should transition from their on-premise solutions to Cloud-based offerings and whether they should consider a platform like Force.com to enable that transition. In their book, authors Alok and Ian explain not just the technology considerations - and common misconceptions -involved in building Cloud Computing applications on Force.com, but more importantly emphasize the need to understand the new business model and commercial viability of Cloud offerings. I found several insights and recommendations that at first glance appear to go against conventional wisdom but turned out to be very practical and relevant to the context. For example, the authors do not recommend an Agile Development Methodology to develop a multi-tenant Force.com application. They warn ISVs that they may not have a viable product business if 30% to 40% of their revenues come from consulting services. The book contains dozens of great questions to consider for the business and technology folks organized into separate sections for easy reference. A very timely book by well-respected veterans, Alok and Ian, who have practical experience with Cloud Computing and the Force.com platform. Highly recommended.

**Kamesh Pemmaraju, Director of Cloud Research, The SandHill Group**

*www.sandhill.com*

# Authors

## Alok Misra

Alok Misra is a Cofounder & Principal at *Navatar Group*, a global Cloud service provider. *Navatar's* long & varied association with *salesforce.com* – as Consulting Partner, OEM Partner, VAR and Vendor – has helped him shape the ideas presented in this book. Alok's market-centric perspective has driven Navatar's commercial success as a Force.com reseller in financial services. He has also been instrumental in creating Navatar's advisory services practice to help ISVs build, launch, sell and support commercial Cloud products.

Alok spent his early career in senior roles at *Deloitte Consulting* and *PricewaterhouseCoopers*. In addition to driving the go-to-market strategy for Navatar and other ISV clients, he writes for several Cloud publications and blogs.

## Ian Gotts

Founder and CEO of Nimbus, which has been offering their business process management solution as a Cloud Computing offering to major corporations including *Toyota, Chevron, Nestlé, HM Revenue & Customs* and *HSBC Bank* for the last 4 years.

They have been a proactive customer of salesforce.com for the last 7 years and have extended it using Force.com to support every area of Nimbus' global operation; sales, support, customer self service, HR, finance, service delivery and R&D. He is the author of 6 books including, *Common Approach, Uncommon Results, Why Killer Products Don't Sell* and two *Thinking of...* books on Cloud Computing. He is a prolific blogger with a rare ability to make the complex seem simple which makes him a sought after and entertaining conference speaker.

# Acknowledgements

Authors are driven to write books for a variety of reasons, but, there is one common theme "the support of others." This is our chance to say thank you.

- To the team of mainly unsung heroes who have worked tirelessly over the years to create and launch Force.com. Without you, there would be no need for this book.
- To Parker Harris for taking the time to write the Foreword and Gordon Evans for facilitating all the support we needed from salesforce.com.
- To those who have reviewed the book during its journey to life and provided candid feedback and real world insights.
- To Stephen Parker who allowed many of the questions from his Thinking of.. Cloud books to be used.
- To David Dobrin, of B2B Analysts, for his insights and edits to the manuscript.
- To the team at Navatar Group for providing the perspective from the trenches – in particular to Ketan Khandkar for the comprehensive architecture questions and to Shweta Kumar, Rexlo Joe, Allan Siegert and Aurobindo Sarkar for validating concepts.
- To everyone at Navatar and Nimbus for the innovative work on Force.com that helped us gain valuable "outside the comfort zone" experience.
- To our friends and families, who have put up with the late nights and lost weekends.

# Foreword

Cloud computing is the white-hot topic in
information technology and salesforce.com is the
leader in enterprise cloud computing. It's
incredible to consider, especially since when we
started in 1999, the term cloud computing wasn't
even used. We didn't have much in those early
days: just a rented apartment as an office, a server
stored in a closet, and a small group of developers
(sleep deprived and living on beef jerky). What we
did have, though, made up for what we lacked.
We were motivated by a vision to change the
software industry, and we had a simple idea about how to make it
more democratic.

Businesses drastically needed more efficient and economical
enterprise software, and once customers were experiencing success
with our CRM application, we realized that we could achieve
something even more significant. What if we made our platform
available to let others build their own cloud apps? The idea to offer
our platform as a service was also a way to resolve our own
problem: customers were demanding more apps, and we couldn't
build everything ourselves. But - more importantly, and something
that as an engineer I could truly appreciate - it offered an
opportunity to change the landscape for anyone who created
applications.

There was so much that was arduous about software development.
(If you haven't been there, trust me; I was one of those sleep-
deprived developers.) There were the purchases: networking
devices, storage systems, databases, app servers, data centers. Then
we had to write the software and ensure it was fast, high quality,
mobile and above all scaled for the Internet. There were
technology issues to address, such as authentication and availability.
It seemed as if the to-do list never ended.

Opening up our platform, Force.com, for others to build upon made development far less complex and less expensive. In fact, research by Nucleus demonstrates that developers using Force.com can achieve results five times faster and at half the cost of traditional platforms. Now with a browser and a Web connection, anyone can build applications and deploy them to users anywhere. People can use these services on whatever they want and all the intellectual property from the first click to the last line of code is stored, tested, deployed, and run in the cloud.

This revolution is generating enthusiasm from independent software vendors, consultants, and internal IT departments who appreciate how platforms remove barriers to innovation and enable them to allocate resources more efficiently. Force.com customers and partners have created more than 160,000 custom applications on our service. They are producing apps in areas of business we didn't even know existed. If you don't believe me take a look at the AppExchange.

Developers constantly have new expectations for how things should work - and they should. Force.com, which incorporates our new collaboration tool, Chatter, also evolves with the shifts underway in the industry. We understand that we in the midst of transitioning from Cloud 1 to Cloud 2 (to touch over click, video over chat, push over pull, tablet over desktop), and these changes don't allow the repurposing of old software, but require writing everything new. Force.com, the complete, collaborative and trusted cloud platform, allows developers to create Cloud 2 apps that are social, real-time, and available on mobile devices. Soon, a new generation of wildly innovative apps that improve productivity, communication, entertainment, and education, will be available on mobile devices and will change entire industries.

By putting the power of application development firmly in the hands of business users, Force.com has changed the application development environment. And it is the users - our customers and partners - who have inspired us most. We have been energized and directed by their passion, enthusiasm, and ingenuity. Companies like FinancialForce.com, with its cloud based accounting package, have recognized the business opportunity to use the Force.com platform.

Large established global ISVs like CA Technologies and BMC Software are using Force.com to launch their cloud computing offerings. Japan Post, the world's largest institution in terms of asset holdings, used the platform to write customer service and regulatory compliance software for more than 75,000 users. The Schumacher Group, a $300 million emergency department and hospital medicine management company in Lafayette, Louisiana, used our platform to build 90 percent of its operational applications and did so four times faster than conventional programs. It also saved resources: If they weren't using the Force.com platform, they would have had to hire an additional five full-time employees.

While there were a number of outspoken cloud critics in our early days, cloud computing is now at a tipping point. Today every major analyst firm sees cloud computing expanding its share of the overall IT market. Gartner Group predicts that cloud computing will continue to be the top strategic opportunity in technology this year, and it forecasts that cloud revenue will grow to $150 billion in 2013. The Software-as-a-Service market is growing twice as fast as the enterprise software market. And, the potential impact of this revolution is astounding. Nicholas Carr, author and one of the influential thinkers in the IT industry, has suggested that "utility-supplied" computing will have economic and social impacts as profound as the ones that took place one hundred years ago, when companies "stopped generating their own power with steam engines and dynamos and plugged into the newly built electric grid." [1]

In the coming decade, thanks to the proliferation of cloud services, ubiquitous, low-cost bandwidth, and cheaper access devices like smartphones and tablets, there will be fewer obstacles than ever. While the opportunity in the cloud is limitless as the Internet, it's difficult to succeed without the proper preparation. Market analysis, business planning, business and technical design, sales and delivery are still critical activities. This book is your key to unlocking success in the cloud as it provides all of the strategic guidance ISVs need.

---

[1] Nicholas Carr, The Big Switch: Rewiring the World, from Edison to Google, New York: Norton, 2008.

The "Smart Questions" structure will help you to make well-informed choices. Nothing is left unexamined: Misra and Gotts explore the issues from both business and technical perspectives, but focus on the one intent that matters most: commercial success on Force.com.

We love the role we have had in evangelizing the industry and the part we play in defining its future direction. We're also aware that that comes with responsibility. We need to set and meet the highest standards of reliability, security and flexibility of any Cloud platform. We believe we are delivering on that promise.

When we started building Salesforce, we were guided by a simple mantra: "do it fast, simple, and right the first time." We knew that the initial prototype set the foundation for the entire product and would determine its ability to scale. These early days matter in your future success. Starting by reading this book and making a commitment to stay close to your customers will get you off to the right start. At salesforce.com, it was our relentless focus on our customers and their success that has shaped our company. It was responding to their needs that helped me make choices. It will be no different for you and I hope you also experience the success that comes in return.

We wish you luck, and we look forward to hearing from you. It's people like you - developing new innovation in the trenches - who inspire us, and who ultimately determine the next phase of this evolution.


*Parker Harris*

*Cofounder, executive vice president, salesforce.com*

# Who should read this book?

## People like you and me

People like you and me should read this book. Although covering a leading edge area of the IT industry this book is not a technical guide, nor was it ever intended to be.

This book is aimed squarely at the Independent Software Vendor (ISV) who is considering Force.com as a route to market their software offerings. Alternatively you could be part of a corporate IT department looking to deliver solutions more quickly for your business users. You have many of the same issues as the ISV, but from a slightly different perspective.

This book is intended to be a catalyst for action aimed at a range of people inside and outside your organization. Here are just a few, and why it is relevant to them:

### Chief Executive Officer

As CEO you are responsible for the overall performance of the business. That means setting the business strategy. You are probably watching with interest the debate around Cloud Computing as a term, and in particular the growing interest in the Force.com platform.

If you are heading up an ISV you can bet that your customers are looking at it as an option to increase availability, increase flexibility or reduce cost.

Understanding the Smart Questions will allow you to formulate your strategy to migrate your solutions into the Cloud.

### Chief Executive Officer of a start-up

You are probably looking at Force.com as a way of getting to market quickly and effectively. Is it the right long term strategy? What are the risks inherent in this strategy? Will it support or hamper your speed to market and your longer term growth?

This book will help you ask the Smart Questions, because if you don't it may cost you the company.

## Chief Technical Officer

You have seen several technology fads come and go. You have already created a plan to move your products to the Cloud and have considered Force.com as a conduit. What is the best design to take advantage of Force.com? What are the issues with developing on a proprietary platform and how do you mitigate those risks?

Asking the Smart Questions will help you assess whether Force.com is the right platform.

## Chief Information Officer / Chief Technical Officer of a corporation

You have formulated a strategy which sets out how IT supports the changing needs of your business organization. Does Force.com change that and make you tear it up and start over – or does it support it?

Although this book highlights all the issues that an ISV may face, several of them may still be relevant to you.

## Head of Development

You deliver stable software as regular controlled releases. It's not always exciting. You are not paid to be exciting. You're paid to be calm and collected. Is Force.com going to change that, and how? What are the issues with developing on Force.com and how do you plan around them?

This book will help you understand what is required, and how you can benefit from Force.com.

## Chief Financial Officer

Everyone claims that Force.com will reduce the cost of ownership of the products. Is that true or are there hidden costs? Are the risks of being tied to salesforce.com outweighed by the benefits? What are the cash flow and funding implications?

This book will give you a sound understanding of the areas to question.

## Investor

So you've invested in an interesting company who is now embarking on a strategy based on Force.com. Is it a clever move or the beginning of the end? How do you evaluate their business plans and budgets? How can you offer the best advice and support?

This book offers the Smart Questions you need to ask to help you assess the impact of Force.com.

## How to use this book

This book is intended to be the catalyst for action. We hope that the ideas and examples presented in this book will inspire you to act. So, do whatever you need to do to make this book useful. Use Post-it notes, write on it, rip it apart, or read it quickly in one sitting. Whatever works for you. We hope this becomes your most dog-eared book.

## Clever clogs – skip to the questions

Some of you will have a deeper understanding of the background of salesforce.com, Force.com and Cloud Computing in general. We still recommend reading Chapters 1 through 3 to see if you can relate to some of the issues that we see companies struggling with. There is also some information on salesforce.com that will be useful, before you skip to the Smart Questions.

# Getting Involved

## The Smart Questions community

There may be questions that we should have asked, but, didn't. There may be specific questions that are relevant to your situation, but, not everyone in general. Go to the website for the book and post the questions. You never know, they may make it into the next edition of the book. This is a key part of the Smart Questions Philosophy.

## Send us your feedback

We love feedback. We prefer great reviews, but, we'll accept anything that helps take the ideas further. We welcome your comments on this book.

We'd prefer email, as it's easy to answer and saves trees. If the ideas worked for you, we'd love to hear your success stories. Maybe we could turn them into a 'Talking Heads'-style video or audio interviews on our website, so others can learn from you. That's one of the reasons why we wrote this book. So talk to us.

*feedback@Smart-Questions.com*

You can also write to the authors at:

*amisra@navatargroup.com*

*ian.gotts@nimbuspartners.com*

## Got a book you need to write?

Maybe you are a domain expert with knowledge locked up inside you. You'd love to share it and there are people out there desperate for your insights. But you don't think you are an author and don't know where to start. Making it easy for you to write a book is part of the Smart Questions Philosophy.

Let us know about your book idea, and let's see if we can help you get your name in print.

*potentialauthor@Smart-Questions.com*

# Table of Contents

**Chapter**

**1**

# Seemed so easy

*In the business world, the rearview mirror is always clearer than the windshield.*

**Warren Buffett (Investor, 1930 - )**

LOOKING at the resignation letter on my desk, I don't understand how we got it so wrong. He was our top salesman and was the most vocal about offering a Cloud solution alongside our existing product. Now he's joining our biggest competitor, who hasn't even considered the Cloud. Why?

Execution was clearly the issue. The strategy was correct, but, our implementation was a disaster. New issues kept surprising us. We underestimated how this new offering would confuse customers. We thought they understood Cloud Computing. However, it simply stalled sales. They assumed they needed less consulting support and projects started to fail. The help desk was swamped and customer satisfaction scores went through the floor.

The worst was the sales cannibalization and changing salesmen's compensation to be tied into our annuity model. That, it seems, was the last straw for our salesmen. If they can't make money, they will go somewhere where they can.

Before we launched our Cloud Computing strategy, 12 months ago, we were at the top of our game. Now we are fighting for survival.

There are so many questions, with hindsight, we wish we'd asked.

## Storm Clouds

A fundamental shift in computing has arrived with the Cloud. It is a reset, changing the dynamics of the industry; the business model, the market leaders, the customer/vendor relationship, and the customers' internal relationships between the line of business and IT. It brings, for once, a big opportunity for smaller vendors and start-ups to level the playing field and join the party. For the bigger players it presents a significant challenge since they need to protect their turf while not letting a great opportunity pass them by. That is the opportunity to enter markets that weren't accessible or even existed before.

Here's the big issue. Most ISVs, established and start-ups, find it extremely challenging to build a business in the Cloud. After spending all the effort and investors cash, many do not see the return on investment. Why?

Let's look at some of these case studies of ISVs that have struggled, to understand why. We have provided eight real cases:

Case 1: Unrealistic ROI expectations

Case 2: Building a consulting practice instead of a product

Case 3: Product development may not need to be agile

Case 4: Cloud - competitive advantage or a barrier to purchase?

Case 5: Unlikely competitors

Case 6: Blind-sided by the cost of upgrades

Case 7: A good Salesforce implementation isn't a viable commercial app

Case 8: Rapid deployment does not mean rapid implementation

So let's look at the gory details of these stories so that we can learn from their pain.

## Case 1: Unrealistic ROI expectation

"We've estimated that we should be able to sell 50,000 to 70,000 subscribers in 3 years," asserted the CEO of a start-up that wanted to build a Force.com app for a vertical market. They assumed that, with 70,000 subscriptions at a price of $125 per month, they'd bring in over $100 million in revenue in their third year. Pretty aggressive!

Now let's look at the CEO's cost model. To build their product, they had hired a programmer with 5 years experience who had dabbled with Apex in a previous job. The programmer had convinced the CEO that he could launch the first version of the app if he received some help from a skilled company in developing the more complex pieces. Together, they estimated the total cost of launching the product at $150k. This included the programmer's salary. They assumed that once they had a basic version, the programmer would be able to continue enhancing it.

The overall estimated cost was $500k per year – against revenue of $100 million. Do you see a problem with this model?[2]

## Case 2: Building a consulting practice instead of a product

"I hold you responsible for not telling me earlier that this would cost so much," yelled the EVP of Product Development at the consultants that were helping him launch a Cloud offering. He was right about the cost spinning out of control. However, he and his team never really paid attention to the advice they were given. As far as the EVP was concerned, his team had been in IT product development for years and had the business knowledge as well as the technical caliber to pull it off. He wanted complete internal ownership of the project - the consultants were just there to help with a few tricky items on the fringes, so their advice was largely ignored.

Things started heading south after the first two potential customers continued to demand more features in the product before they paid a cent. Then came the expectations related to performance and more advanced features. The expectations kept mounting. Within

---

[2] If it looks too good to be true – it probably is.

the next few months, a significant number of the product team members got involved in figuring out how to meet the rapidly escalating demands from the first set of buyers.

Mired in product features and attributes, the product team didn't realize that they were getting into a consulting role with their potential customers – but, that was also something they weren't trained to do. They didn't know how to manage the scope of work or customer expectations. They had no idea how to push back so they continued accepting all demands and suggestions, turning the product scope into a constantly moving target.

The EVP went to the CFO for more funding and the executive team was appalled. They had already spent upwards of $2 million and it seemed like a bottomless pit with no revenue in sight anywhere. The executives pulled the plug on the entire initiative.

## Case 3: Product development may not need to be agile

The application was meant for employees to book their vacations. It seemed simple. Basically, you need an employee record and for each employee a vacation record with a start date and end date. Sound easy, right?

Now let's take a closer look at the problem. There are actually 12 types of leave. Some paid, some unpaid. What happens if you book leave and are not entitled to it? Or book it and don't take it? Or take it and need a salary sacrifice?

As you start digging deeper, you uncover more scenarios like these that require more thinking as well as consensus building. However, the common excuse (or claim) is that you don't need to be rigorous in understanding requirements in the Cloud model - you can use agile development approaches so that you can build as you go.

Now let's add another dimension to this problem - deployment. Your app is multi-tenant – it is being used by 100 companies (customers). Every time you discover and develop something new, you now have to roll it out to all of these customers. Think of all the issues involved – upgrading, testing, training, support for all of these customers. More importantly, a big assumption you may be making is that the design of your Cloud app permits you to roll out frequent changes and additions.

That is simply misguided. Your product must be multi-tenant in order for you to have a viable Cloud business. The concept of multi-tenancy is a bit similar to a condo building with multiple tenants. After a building is populated with tenants, it isn't easy to replace the core structure of the building on an ad hoc basis; similarly it is not easy to replace the application architecture of a Cloud product after it is rolled out to customers. However, you can expand on it, if the foundation is solid.

To build a solid foundation, you cannot ignore the core principles of custom software development when developing on Force.com – in fact, they become even more critical. The first activity is still to lock down as much of the requirements as possible, in process or operational terms. Once you have a good handle on your entire set of requirements and the end user processes, you will create the object model and architecture for your app. It is critical to get this right before you get anywhere near coding[3].

## Case 4: Cloud - competitive advantage or a barrier to purchase?

Cloud is the next big thing. It is the future. Just look at salesforce.com's revenue growth. The business case looked cast iron. The product team worked hard to identify the new application space and the R&D team worked miracles and the new application was brought to market in record time.

In the customer user groups the new application got the thumbs up. When the sales team started to take it to their customers early sales took off. The business users loved the new functionality and the flexibility to access the data from anywhere. This is the power of the Cloud.

Initial pilots were sold, with a high cost of sale due to the support required to get customers onboard. The pilots were successful, but then the problems started. The profitable larger roll-outs did not come. "The only one with more pilots than us is South West Airlines," said an exasperated CEO. "We've invested heavily in the Cloud and I need to see a return."

---

[3] But the Force.com platform is so compelling and you just want to start building. Sit in a small windowless room until that feeling passes.

What were the reasons for the delays? There were questions about the location of the data, audits of the data center's security, back-up/restore and disaster recovery. The final straw was the difficulty integrating with each of the customer's existing infrastructure. Much of this was masking the emotional response from the customer's IT organization – "This is outsourcing by stealth."

It eventually became clear that the sector the application was aimed at was not ready for the Cloud. It wasn't 'No never' but 'No now.' Probably, given several years when Cloud offerings are more mature and ubiquitous, then the sector might be more open. That doesn't help the ISV that has invested time and money bringing a product to market. Worse, they had potentially cannibalized or stalled sales of the existing on-premise product having shown business users a glimpse of the future.

"Deep research into a paradigm shifting product's potential market is probably more valuable than anything else. These are expensive lessons," concluded the CEO at the annual investor's conference.

## Case 5: Unlikely competitors

"Sorry this has taken a bit longer than we anticipated," said the Account Executive during his weekly call with the VP-Sales. He had been working on three deals for the past two months. All of these deals were related to the new Cloud version of their product, which had taken around 12 months and $700k to develop. The ISV had a solid technical team that had been through all the required trainings, certifications and researched all the technical options.

The technical team carved out a set of requirements using the product managers of the on-premise product, hired some Force.com developers and delivered the first version of the product in 12 months, slightly longer than the anticipated 8 months. The Business Development guys had signed an OEM Partner Agreement with salesforce.com, so the ISV could resell Force.com seats bundled with their Cloud product. Now the Cloud product was ready for primetime and all eyes were on the sales team to deliver.

The sales team had always been used to a 6-9 month sales cycle for their on-premise version of the product, which sold for half a million dollars. However, the projected combined first-year revenue from the sales of the Cloud version from these three deals was only around $15,000. They also found that the effort required to make the sale was the same as the on-premise version, despite the extremely low revenue numbers. The Account Executive and the VP were both concerned about their commissions. They wondered about the long term viability of a model where the revenue numbers were very low whereas the effort required to close every deal was still the same.

There was something else that puzzled the VP-Sales. The Account Executive had just learned that their main competitor, on two of the three deals, was the salesforce.com direct sales rep who, in partnership with a salesforce.com implementation partner, was positioning a Force.com Enterprise License Agreement so the prospects could custom-build all of their apps they needed.

The ISV sales team was in a bind. Would they have to now figure out how to come up with a better value proposition and pricing to compete with their partner salesforce.com? Would they now have to unbundle the Force.com seats from their Cloud product, let the salesforce.com direct sales rep sell his deals first, and then sell their own product as a plug in? Would they now have to start thinking about building a consulting practice for implementation and customization of salesforce.com products? Would they have to build other relationships that they hadn't thought of before? It all seemed like too much work for too little revenue!

## Case 6: Blind-sided by the cost of upgrades

The start-up had done really well in their first year. They started with $500k of seed money, and the talented technical team launched the first version of the workflow management product in 8 months. Their CEO, well connected in the technology world, brought in the first sales. They had 10 customers with around 120 subscribers in just 4 months. Although they were only collecting $20 per subscriber each month, things seemed upbeat. After all, they had the product already and all they needed were more customers. They projected adding 1500 subscribers in the next two years. They hired two more salespeople and began ramping up the back office team as well.

The trouble began when their customers started coming to them asking for more features. It seemed that another salesforce.com partner had also launched a competing offering. The start-up had to act fast. Their technical team worked with the customers, compiled a list of all new features/functions required and came back to the CEO with the game plan. The underlying object model and design of the product would have to be changed to accommodate the new features. It would take around 6 months to develop and roll out, they estimated. However, the catch was that there was no way to roll out an upgrade to existing customers due to the changes in the object model. Each existing customer would have to be migrated to the new version. Each migration for a customer was expected to take 3-4 weeks and would cost around $20k. By the time the new release would be ready, they estimated they'd have 80 customers to migrate, and would therefore need a significant chunk of change to fund that.

Ever the salesman, the CEO assured the team he'd be able to get the customers to pay for the migration. He went and talked to two customers about the plan. They would be getting all the fabulous new features in 6 months – however, they'd have to shell out a one-time $20k fee for the new features. The CEO wasn't prepared for the response. "Why do we have to pay these fees for the new features? Doesn't Cloud Computing mean that we pay you a monthly fee and you figure out the rest?" was the response he received. It became clear to him, after the first few conversations, that the customers wouldn't pay anything for the upgrade. This was an unanticipated cost which threatened to completely destroy their business plan.

## Case 7: A good Salesforce implementation isn't a viable commercial app

Their Salesforce deployment had been hugely successful. With the help of a consultant the financial services firm had spent 6 months creating a custom app, to manage customers and investments. They used Visualforce and Apex to create great looking custom screens and functionality, which everyone liked. The salesforce.com team was impressed enough to get the firm's CIO on stage at Dreamforce, salesforce.com's annual event, to demonstrate the app.

Several other financial firms attending, came up to the CIO to compliment him on his creation. The firm was beginning to realize that they had created something that everyone else needed. They thought they were sitting on a gold mine and had to figure out how to sell it to other firms looking for a similar solution. The CIO convinced their management that there was a way to package and commercialize the app to sell to others and create a new revenue source. Everyone agreed that the idea had legs.

The CIO spent the next 3-4 months understanding Force.com's packaging technology and talking to several technical experts. He soon realized that they would need outside help and began discussions with several salesforce.com implementation partners. His idea was to pick a salesforce.com partner who would implement the app for others, make some money, and pay royalties to the financial firm. After all, 70% of the work was already done, which would make it easy, he reasoned. A consulting partner was picked and a partnership formed.

A year passed, but, not much happened. The consulting partner found two prospects. However, their needs were a bit different, requiring significant customization. The prospects weren't willing to spend $50k - $80k in customizations. "What's the point of buying a product if we're paying for consulting," they demanded.

It soon became clear that something would need to be done to the financial app to productize it[4], so it could be deployed without customers having to spend too much on customizations. What would that "something" be? How much would it cost? Who would pay for that exercise? Would there be "consulting" dollars for the consulting firm? Who would maintain and support that "something"?

## Case 8: Rapid deployment does not mean rapid *implementation*

"The best thing about Cloud CRM applications is that they are available," says the sales manager. "We just roll it out by sending emails with people's log-on details. Hey presto, done. I don't understand why IT takes so long."

Bored and confused by Siebel, frustrated with inaccurate sales data it produces, the sales manager bought Salesforce CRM. This was under the radar so that their IT department was blissfully unaware.

---

[4] Remember a Cloud ISV still has a product. It is the customer who sees it as a service.

Sales people are dreadful at following process or filling out CRM data, so training was eliminated in the interest of speed. Besides, there was online training provided with the application.

It was bought on Tuesday, implemented on Wednesday. No disruption to the sales team. Brilliant!

So now they had a shiny new system straight out of the box, not tailored for their specific sales process, with no training. It was being used by people who didn't really care about the system apart from entering the minimum data required to get their commissions paid.[5]

A few months later they had a new system full of inaccurate sales data. It was just as useless for managing and forecasting as Siebel was. Why?

The new system did not fit the current sales process exactly so each sales person found workarounds. With no guidance on how to fill out the 'Commission % Due', 'Marketing required' and 'Value of customer' fields every sales person completed them differently, based on their perspective.

"Implementing a new system should have given us a massive opportunity to revisit processes, eliminate non-value added activities, get consistency across the teams, and choose the best practice from the teams. And then we could have implemented those and locked them in with a new system," agonized the sales manager. This required a process-led approach supported by a robust methodology and tools.

Why will the implementation of your Force.com application for your customers be any different? Did you build the flexibility needed to address the process issues for each of your potential customers?

Your success will be dependent on your customer's success.

## So what are they missing?

The examples above are not fiction, they are painfully true. Now let's see what went wrong with each of them:

---

[5] Is that a light at the end of the tunnel or actually a train coming the other way?

Case 1 – Assumed that hiring a good technical skill-set was enough to bring success in the Cloud

Case 2 – Put their product organization into a consultative role of implementing a Cloud app for their customer

Case 3 – Thought that the Cloud stands for build as you go and removes the need for solid architecture and design

Case 4 – Didn't try to understand whether their customers and market were ready for the Cloud

Case 5 – Did not create a realistic sales strategy for the Cloud world

Case 6 – Paid no attention to anything beyond developing version one of their product

Case 7 – Assumed that their own implementation of Salesforce was so great that it could be sold to others

Case 8 – Did not think about what processes had to be supported by the application

The common theme in most of these cases was that they only paid attention to building their product. This is the overarching problem with most ISVs – they get influenced by all the hype. They view the Cloud as just another language or architecture to learn. They join the bandwagon expecting that the cash registers will start ringing once their product is built and launched.

Even when they do come to us for advice, they seldom ask the right questions. All they want to know is: a) *Is Force.com the right platform* and b) *How much would it cost to build our product?*

These questions are good; however, they are only related to product *development*, not *profitability*. It takes much more than just developing your app, if you're looking to build a successful Cloud business.

This book isn't the first one to point out that the Cloud isn't just a technology transition, but, a completely different commercial model. In fact, there are some differences that are so critical that they will actually dictate whether you will succeed or fail. In most of the cases that we highlighted, the companies did not understand these differences. For instance, the differences between:

• Selling a product versus delivering a service

- Creating a multi-tenant model versus a single tenant model
- Product revenue versus consulting revenue
- Implementing Salesforce versus developing a commercial Cloud product
- Building in a public Cloud versus an on premise platform

You will learn more about these differences, and how they can impact your business, in the later chapters.

You're right to get excited about the potential that Force.com offers. However, simply building an app on Force.com is not like winning the lottery. If you don't ask the right questions up front to understand the Cloud business model, you could be writing checks for years, without seeing any return.

# Chapter 2

# The future is here

*When I stop learning something new and start talking about the past versus the future, I will go.*

**Jack Welch (Former Chairman, General Electric, 1935 – )**

TEN years ago the only IT a person used was the one that their company gave them. Now the applications and tools, disguised as websites, that people access outside their work life are setting expectations for enterprise applications. They expect at work the look and feel, speed, location independence and, finally the range of devices that they can use at home.

Enterprise applications are often far more constrained and robust due to the need for scalability, security and the complex integrations with other parts of the infrastructure. To the business user this just seems like excuses for IT not delivering. More than ever, business users are willing to subscribe to Cloud services from outside vendors, bypassing their IT altogether.

Last year *Information Age* highlighted 10 Cloud Computing business success stories. What is interesting is they are all using the Cloud equivalent of packaged applications. You could argue that *Japan Post* is the exception as they are using a Cloud platform – Force.com – to extend the core CRM and build applications.

---

## Information Age business success stories

Information Age listed its view of some of the business success stories, and here they are:

**Japan Post**: Using Force.com they developed a data consolidation system in 3 months and rolled it out to 65,000 users in 24,000 branches.

**Santander Consumer Finance**: Uses Service-Now.com IT Service Management at a fraction of the cost of their previous on-premise application.

**Roche**: Adopted a Cloud Computing talent management service from Taleo dramatically improving its reputation with potential graduate candidates.

**GE**: Managing 50,000 suppliers using multiple apps was a challenge, so when they wanted to consolidate they chose Aravo as it supported the scale GE needed.

**ACAL Technology**: While reorganizing their international sales operation decided to provide better tools for office and field team and chose NetSuite.

**Osborne Clarke**: The law firm's E-mail service was under attack, so they implemented Mimecast, which was significantly cheaper than an in-house alternative.

**Abbot Medical Optics**: To improve the visibility of its expense management they turned to Concur as they could cope with the multi-country tax complexity.

**Chiquita**: Its legacy HR could not cope with the scale of operation; 24,000 employees in 70 countries. Workday beat off the on-premise offerings.

**Thomas Cook**: RightNow's CRM system was so friendly, it was the choice for the single customer service bank, for their call centre and home-based agents.

**THK-BP**: Reducing contract approval from 12 hours to 6, and reducing admin overhead was a key benefit of implementing OILspace Energy Trade Risk app.

---

As you can see, the Cloud has opened up a huge opportunity for both ISVs and corporations. For a buyer (corporation), the "rental" opportunity to pay for monthly usage of a service through the internet instead of spending millions on buying software and hardware, and then maintaining it. For you, the seller (or ISV) it's a mechanism to establish a recurring revenue model, once you sell to a customer.

It seems like a win-win situation, so why not jump in with both feet, you're wondering. You have decades of technology experience already, as well as programmers who can be retrained on the Force.com platform. Build your app in the Cloud and begin to rock'n'roll.

---

That is not a given, as we pointed out in the previous chapter. It's ironic that even though the demand for Cloud-based apps is increasing, most established software companies have been unable to take advantage of it.

## New type of business

Ultimately a shift from on premise solutions to Cloud-based solutions has far less to do with technology than with getting into an entirely different type of business.

From a technical point of view, a move towards Cloud Computing is a move towards commoditization and outsourcing of some aspects of IT. When something becomes well enough understood and capable of automation, humans can be removed from the process. Provisioning servers, installing software on them, setting up network addresses, routes and firewalls all now fall within this category. You now have the opportunity to replace all of this by Force.com's infrastructure, and let salesforce.com manage it for you. Sounds good, right?

From a business standpoint, however, it poses a new set of challenges. Cloud Computing will be attractive to your buyers *because they will be paying you much less and spreading payments over a longer period of time.*[6]

Therein lays the problem. It means that you will have to do everything to please your customers on an ongoing basis, but, they will pay you a tiny fraction of what you would have gotten as an on premise software vendor.

"But wait a minute - won't I have to do less in the Cloud since someone else maintains the infrastructure?" you're asking. Yes that's true. But then you will be spending your time doing things for your customers that you wouldn't have done in an on premise model, which will probably offset any gains from outsourcing your infrastructure. You will become like a landlord with your tenants expecting you to keep things in top shape in exchange for a low monthly rent.

The reality is that the cost of developing and maintaining your product, as well as managing your customers, will turn out to be

---

[6] HINT: This is the point where you get *less* excited

much higher than expected. Without the high one-time on premise product license sale, you will have to significantly ramp up sales of your Cloud product. It will be a different business model and a tough proposition.

## Should you be your greatest competitor?

Now that you know it won't be a slam dunk, the big question is, "Will you obsolete your on-premise product with one developed on a Cloud platform, or will someone else?" It may be that you have no choice other than diving into the Cloud. On the other hand adopting a "watching brief" or building some new defensive partnerships could be the right approach. What you cannot do is have no position at all, bury your head in the sand and hope it all goes away.

It also depends on what is happening in your business and your market. There are so many unanswered questions that determine whether the Cloud is a "go" or a "no-go."

Let's begin with a basic understanding of the Cloud layers.

## The Cloud Layers

Salesforce.com may have raised people's understanding of what is possible from the Cloud and themselves, but now there is no shortage of players now offering some variant of the Cloud to customers.

They are not all the same. This is only making it more complicated for potential ISVs, who are looking to leverage the investments of these Cloud players.

It is generally accepted that the vendors are stratifying into 3 layers: *Apps*, which sit on a *Platform*, which requires *Infrastructure*. The diagram on the next page is by no means exhaustive, but, it starts to show some of the players in each layer.

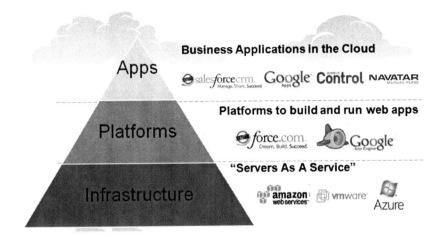

# The confusion

Not everything in the Cloud world is as neatly stacked as the diagram above suggests. Since this is all so new, an apples-to-apples comparison between two Cloud platforms such as Force.com and Azure may also be extremely hard. This is because each of the vendors, in their quest for gaining market share, is also defining the value proposition of a Cloud platform. For instance, one platform may offer you embedded CRM features, while another may provide the ability to retain your existing programming talent. One vendor may be raving about multi-tenancy, while another may be listing the virtues of owning your Cloud.

What makes it even harder is that there are very few examples of companies that have been raking in money after building commercial apps on a third party public Cloud platform. There are very few role models to emulate. Consulting firms selling services in the Cloud are adding to the confusion, leading ISVs away from the product path towards a consultative model.

In most of the companies discussed in the cases in Chapter 1, there were no shortages of technical talent – they had a pretty good handle on the features, functions and widgets available through Force.com. They just didn't know how to *monetize* their investment.[7]

---

[7] Tom Cruise was right in the film Jerry Maguire when he said "Show me the money"

The future is here

# Salesforce.com & Force.com

*It's a lot easier just to write big checks than it is to innovate.*

**Marc Benioff (Chairman & CEO, salesforce.com, 1964 - )**

S ALESFORCE.COM has been at the vanguard of Cloud Computing. It was the poster child for Cloud CRM. However, it has evolved beyond that. It started with the ability to customize the name of a tab, such as changing 'Account' to 'Customer', then the ability to extend the CRM application. It is now an entire development platform in the Cloud called Force.com.

At a very basic level, salesforce.com has exposed the building blocks that they used to build the Salesforce CRM application and branded it Force.com. Simple, but inspired[8].

## Where does Force.com fit?

Force.com has now proven to be the 'secret sauce' for salesforce.com. It has made the CRM application stickier by providing an enterprise the ability to build extensions for a closer fit with the business. This drives up adoption which in turn reduces churn.

But you can build entire applications which have nothing to do with CRM using Force.com.

---

[8] But then again the simple things often are.

After you have built them, you can sell them to other companies and make money from them. You can develop an entire software business without actually having to maintain infrastructure.

That is what this book is all about.

## Putting it all together

The diagram on the below is a representation of the overall salesforce.com offering, and the core elements at each level.

At the top level, the *Applications* (Sales Cloud and Service Cloud from salesforce.com) sit alongside the applications (Custom Cloud) that anyone can build using Force.com.

These applications run on the *Cloud Platform* which provides the tools for application development using a proprietary programming language called Apex. A runtime engine loads metadata for these applications at execution time.

The Cloud platform requires a *Cloud Infrastructure* to run securely and scale – data centers, servers, operating system, database, internet connectivity and disaster recovery and so on.

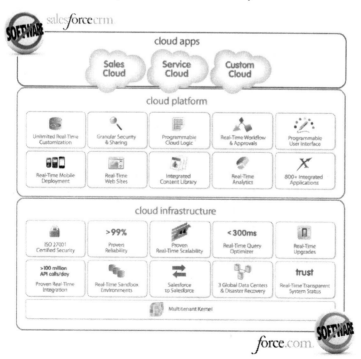

# Taking it apart

What differentiates a true Cloud Computing platform from other wannabes is the concept of multi-tenancy. A multi-tenant architecture is when customers share an app in the Cloud. A single-tenant Cloud app is similar, if not identical, to the old ASP model. Force.com provides the ability for your Cloud product to be multi-tenant – a necessary condition for you to survive and make money in this world as it allows you to service small customers at the same cost as enterprise customers[9].

It is worth understanding some of the key constituents required to develop Force.com applications. These are technical in nature, rather than relating to the core elements in the diagram in the previous section.

This book is not intended to provide detailed and up-to-date information on Force.com development. You can probably get into more depth on these constituents by visiting the site: *www.developer.force.com*. However, we mention them here for those of you that are completely new to the Force.com world.

## Application Framework

The Application Framework lets you customize existing applications or build applications from scratch. It is a drag and drop application builder, or in marketing-techno speak "You can use the declarative power of the Application Framework to quickly create robust applications on Force.com."

The Application Framework Builder gives you easy-to-use tools to modify your data structure, as well as to specify the scope of applications or the layout of data on a page. You can also define workflows based on user interaction with data or create reports on the data. You can use buttons or custom links to extend the default capabilities of your Force.com application. You can create and modify tabs which can be associated with a Force.com object, Visualforce page, s-control or any web page. You can give users

---

[9] This is called the Long Tail, a term brought into mainstream awareness by Chris Anderson's book, The Long Tail.

access to tabs, and the users can customize the display of their own set of tabs within an application.[10]

## Web Services API

The Force.com Web Services API provides access to your Force.com data and logic. You can call the Web Services API from a wide variety of client-side languages. All of the functionality built into the Force.com platform is automatically part of any application that uses the Web Services API. Data validation, workflow, Apex triggers and the Force.com security schema are just a few of the features that help you to integrate your external application with the Force.com platform.

## Apex Code

Force.com Apex Code is a strongly-typed programming language that executes on the Force.com platform. Apex is used to add business logic to applications, to write database triggers, and to program controllers in the user interface layer. It is tightly integrated with the database and query language, provides good web services support, and includes features for execution in a multi-tenant environment.

## Visualforce

At the front of any great business application is a great user interface; easy to use, powerful and suited exactly for the tasks, users and devices the application serves. Force.com's Visualforce provides a complete framework for building and deploying any kind of user experience, enabling any kind of interface design and interaction to be built and delivered entirely on demand. These user interfaces can extend the standard Force.com look and feel, or replace it with a completely unique style and set of sophisticated interactions, thus allowing the power of Platform-as-a-Service to be extended to virtually any requirement.

## Database Services

Data is the foundation of all information systems and Database Services are the foundation for applications created on Force.com. Force.com Database Services allow you to create objects to store

---

[10] And a whole lot more in every new release of Force.com

all of your data, letting the enterprise power of the platform handle the difficult task of ensuring that your data is safe and continually available.

Database Services go far beyond simple storage of data. The entire functionality of Database Services is available to all applications running on Force.com, whether they are built with the declarative application framework, extended with Force.com Apex Code and Visualforce Pages, or simply accessing data through the Force.com Web Services API.

## Packaging

Packages provide you with a powerful way to distribute your applications to your customers. Packages are like suitcases that can contain your components, code or apps. You can use a package to bundle something as small as an individual component or as large as a set of related apps.

Packages come in two forms, managed and unmanaged. Unmanaged packages can be used for a one time distribution to one or more customers, like a template. Managed packages are ideal when building an app with plans to upgrade. You can continue to upgrade the managed packages after they've been deployed.

## Other capabilities

Salesforce.com has also recently launched Chatter, the collaboration Cloud, which has been getting a lot of attention. Depending on your target audience, Chatter may be a useful tool for your Force.com app, for Facebook type collaboration within the enterprise.

What gets little attention is something we have found to be very useful for many types of apps; the built-in reporting engine that comes with Force.com which is very powerful and easy to use.

Force.com Sites allows public web sites to be a part of your product. So users think that they are interacting with a website, but are actually populating your app with data. With everything hosted on salesforce.com's Cloud, this can be a very powerful feature.

These are capabilities that may or may not be useful depending on the customer segment you will be serving.

## What about the company?

Like most successful Silicon Valley technology companies, salesforce.com had very humble beginnings. It was started in a small rented apartment in San Francisco. It's surely come a long way. As salesforce.com transitions from the hottest start-up with a cool product, to the industry leader that most companies want to partner or compete with, its internal culture assumes more significance.

Marc Benioff's long association with Oracle helped attract a lot of talent from the tech giant. While the strong focus on innovation helped build a motivated workforce, the deep Oracle roots defined how the company worked with its customers and partners. Salesforce.com built a partner ecosystem of companies that provided complementary products and services. However, the core offering continued to be sold directly by the salesforce.com sales teams.

For its next phase of growth, salesforce.com is looking to recruit OEM partners and Value Added Resellers (VARs) – companies that will build their products on the Force.com platform and sell a bundled offering. If you build your product on Force.com, you may have a choice to be a part of this indirect channel. Of course, you may also choose to sell your product separately as a plug-in and let the salesforce.com direct sales rep sell the Force.com seats.

In most cases, you will be dealing with various groups within salesforce.com. You are most likely to interact with the following:

**ISV Alliance Manager** – Part of the Channels organization, your Alliance Manager may become your overall point of contact at salesforce.com. Their role is to recruit ISV partners, help them through the process of developing the app, and manage the ongoing relationship.

**Platform Evangelist** – Also part of the Channels organization, the Platform Evangelist may be the lead technical resource that you can turn to at salesforce.com.

**AppExchange Manager** – Your AppExchange contact would be someone that you may interact with, if you decide to list your app on AppExchange.

**Partner Marketing Manager** – Although it sounds like someone who can help you market your products to your customers, the Partner Marketing Manager is really someone who is selling sponsorships of salesforce.com events to partners.

**Account Executive** – An Account Executive is a part of the salesforce.com direct sales team, selling to customers. You may run into an Account Executive during the sales process, sometimes in a competitive situation, when you are selling to your customers.

## Where is salesforce.com headed?

After changing the landscape for sales force automation, salesforce.com has successfully opened up the world's eyes to the larger Cloud Computing opportunity. They are the innovator, the market leader, as well as the industry's blue-eyed boy in terms of potential. Since they have executed so well, there is every reason to believe that they will maintain their dominant position, and Force.com will evolve into the Platform as a Service (PaaS) of choice.

However, salesforce.com is still a relatively small company when stacked up against the larger Cloud Computing demand and opportunity. Larger players such as *Microsoft*, *Oracle*, *IBM* and a few others have the incumbent advantage, deeper pockets and wider partner/reseller networks. Salesforce.com has yet to clearly spell out if it wants to go deeper with Sales & Service Clouds using its current direct sales model or wider with the Force.com platform through an indirect sales channel. What happens to Force.com if salesforce.com is acquired?

It is true that Marc Benioff, in his quest for the "end of software", has been instrumental in starting a revolution. "He's shown he can topple an industry – but can he lead one," asks Joshua Weinberger, Managing Editor of CRM Magazine. It remains to be seen whether salesforce.com can maintain the leadership position that it currently enjoys.

As often with any new model, there are too many unanswered questions and risks. However, the opportunity is also too big and too real to ignore. Salesforce.com has helped us to see the opportunity, and forced us to have a discussion about the Cloud.

Despite the risks, doing nothing doesn't seem to be an option for you anymore because Force.com also significantly lowers the barrier to entry for your competition.

## The common misconceptions

That partner ecosystem that salesforce.com built helped them sell Salesforce CRM and make it sticky. The partners were mostly either consultants providing implementation and support services, or ISVs selling add-ons to Salesforce CRM. This group of partners still forms the bulk of the partner ecosystem. For them, the focal point of each engagement is Salesforce CRM sold by the salesforce.com direct sales team in most situations. The sales and partner engagement model that evolved was based on a tight relationship between the partner and the salesforce.com sales and marketing teams.

As an ISV with a Cloud product, where you will be reselling Force.com, your success will be driven by you, not salesforce.com. Your product will have to become the focal point of each sale, with salesforce.com supporting you as your infrastructure provider. This model is different from the model that the earlier salesforce.com partners had been used to. However, the older model, being the dominant model, has created quite a few misconceptions which can threaten the viability of your Cloud business. Here are some of them:

*Myth #1: You can build your Force.com product business at a much lower cost than a product business on other on-premise platforms.* Maybe you can build Version one of your Force.com product at a much lower cost. Turning in a profit will be very challenging in the Cloud commercial model and if you don't get it right, it may empty your wallet fast.

*Myth #2: You should follow the example of a successful consulting partner.* You should, if you want to become a consulting firm in the Cloud. The revenue and go-to-market model of a salesforce.com consulting partner, with the bulk of their revenues coming from services, is very different from what you will need to build.

*Myth #3: Force.com makes your product multi-tenant, so you can manage costs.* Force.com is multi-tenant, but, it doesn't automatically make your product multi-tenant. There's significant thinking and work, both business and technical, that will be required on *your* part to build multi-tenancy at the app level.

**Myth #4**: *It doesn't matter whether your revenues come from products or services, as long as you're in the Cloud.* If more than 30 - 40% of your revenues come from services, your product business won't be viable. You may then try to become a services company, but, you won't be able to provide the margins that your investors will be looking for.

**Myth #5**: *You'll need to find a good Force.com technical architect and write an RFP to pick a consultant.* If you had to switch from Java to .Net, maybe this strategy would have worked. Unfortunately, most companies today follow this approach and build a product, but, don't find more than five paying customers.

**Myth #6**: *Agile Development methodology is the way to develop a good Force.com app.* If you want a multi-tenant product, you will need a more structured approach, where you finalize your app design upfront and follow a tightly managed development process.

**Myth #7**: *You need to be closely aligned with the salesforce.com sales teams.* Salesforce.com sales teams may or may not be a sales channel for you. It's more important to be able to sell your product directly.

**Myth #8**: *You need to emulate the selling model and collateral that the salesforce.com sales team uses.* This would imply that your value proposition is the same as salesforce.com's. Why would anyone buy from you then?

**Myth#9**: *Everyone will buy your Force.com based product from the AppExchange.* If you're building an add-on to Salesforce CRM, they may. In most situations, your prospective customers will find you through forums and circles related to your industry. AppExchange may still be a good marketing tool alongside other approaches.

**Myth#10**: *The first thing to do is build a prototype of our product.* You have to ask yourself what the prototype will help you achieve. The very first thing to figure out may be whether your product will be commercially viable.

## Should we just emulate salesforce.com?

Everyone wants to copy the sales, marketing and development model that salesforce.com adopted, and for good reason. "After all, if they became a billion-plus dollar company using that approach, why don't we just adopt the winning formula," reasoned the CEO of an enterprise software company that was considering building a product on Force.com.

In fact, there's a lot to be learned from salesforce.com's model. Their marketing team is, arguably, the best we have seen in the software world and their sales organization is top notch. Above all, Force.com is their creation so who else would know the ins and outs of the platform better. So go ahead and absorb what you can.

We wish it was all that easy. Emulating every aspect of salesforce.com also has strong disadvantages since your situation will be different from theirs in so many respects. For instance, salesforce.com never had to build and market on a third-party Cloud Computing platform. You will.

# Chapter

# 4

## Ask the Smart Questions

*If I have seen further it is by standing on the shoulders of giants*

**Isaac Newton (Scientist, 1643 – 1727)**

SMART Questions is about giving you valuable insights or "the Smarts". Normally these are only gained through years of painful and costly experience. Whether you already have a general understanding of the subject and need to take it to the next level or are starting from scratch, you need to make sure you ask the Smart Questions. We aim to short circuit that learning process, by providing the expertise of the 'giants' that Isaac Newton referred to.

Not all the questions will necessarily be new or staggeringly insightful. The value you get from the information will clearly vary. It depends on your job role and previous experience. We call this the 3Rs.

---

**The 3 Rs**

Some of the questions will be in areas where you know all the answers so they will be **Reinforced** in your mind.

You may have forgotten certain areas so the book will **Remind** you.

And other questions may be things you've never considered and will be **Revealed** to you.

---

## How do you use Smart Questions?

The structure of the questions is set out in Chapter 5, and the questions are in Chapters 6 and 7. The questions are laid out in a series of structured and ordered tables with the questions in one column and the explanation of why it matters alongside. We've also provided a checkbox so that you can mark which questions are relevant to your particular situation.

A quick scan down the first column in the list of questions should give you a general feel of where you are for each question vs. the 3Rs.

At the highest level they are a sanity check or checklist of areas to consider. You can take them with you to meetings or use as the basis of your ITT. Just one question may save you a whole heap of cash or heartache.

In Chapter 8 we've tried to bring some of the questions to life with some real-life examples.

We trust that you will find real insights. There may be some 'aha' moments. Hopefully not too many sickening, 'head in the hands – what have we done' moments, where you've realized that your company is hopelessly exposed. If you are in that situation, then the questions may help you negotiate yourself back into control.

In this context, probably the most critical role of the questions is that they reveal risks that you hadn't considered. On the flip side they should also open up your thinking to opportunities that you hadn't necessarily considered. Balancing the opportunities and the risks, and then agreeing what is realistically achievable is the key to formulating strategy.

The questions could be used in your internal operational meetings to inform or at least prompt a debate. Alternatively they could shape the discussion you have with potential vendors of Cloud services.

Once that strategy is set, the questions should enable you to develop operational plans, budgets or determine your strategy.

# How to dig deeper

Need more information? Not convinced by the examples, or want ones that are more relevant to you specific situation? You can contact the authors (their email addresses have been provided in the "Getting Involved" section at the beginning of the book). The Smart Questions micro-site for the book has a list of other supporting material. As this is a rapidly advancing subject many of the references are to websites or blogs.

And of course there is a community of people who've read the book and are all at different levels of maturity who have been brought together on the Smart Questions micro-site for the book.

# And finally

Please remember that these questions are NOT intended to be a prescriptive list that must be followed slavishly from beginning to end. It is also inevitable that the list of questions is not exhaustive and we are confident that with the help of the community the list of Smart Questions will grow.

If you want to rephrase a question to improve its context or have identified a question we've missed, then let us know to add to the collective knowledge.

We also understand that not all of the questions will apply to all businesses. However we encourage you to read them all as there may be a nugget of truth that can be adapted to your circumstances.

Above all we do hope that it provides a guide or a pointer to the areas that may be valuable to you and helps with the "3 Rs".

# Chapter

# The known unknowns

*There are known knowns. These are things we know that we know. There are known unknowns. That is to say, there are things that we now know we don't know. But there are also unknown unknowns. These are things we do not know we don't know[11].*

**Donald Rumsfeld (former US Defense Secretary, 1932 - )**

BUILDING your cloud business using Force.com will require a very tight collaboration between your business and technical teams. In most organizations, one leads the other, making joint decision-making harder. In this situation it may be no different. At the minimum, you will need both business and technical executives to be engaged.

Since it's not uncommon for business and technical people to be thinking about very different sets of issues, the questions have been divided into these two sections.

## Chapter 6: Questions for suits

1. Is Cloud Computing for me?
2. Is Force.com the right Cloud Computing platform?
3. Commercial considerations
4. What is your Go to Market strategy?
5. How your organization will need to change?
6. Migrating to the Cloud and Force.com

---

[11] So we are clear then? This statement, made at a press briefing by former US Defense Secretary Donald Rumsfeld, earned him the 2003 Foot in Mouth award from the Plain English Campaign.

## Chapter 7: Questions for jeans

1. The big picture
2. Designing your product
3. Developing your product
4. Deploying your product

Many of the considerations in the business sections are to help you figure out the commercial viability of your Cloud initiative. However, if you are more technically focused, do not automatically skip to the questions for jeans. We do recommend taking a quick look at the questions asked of the business. It will help you understand the context for the technical questions.

Clearly there are technical questions around architecture, development, and support. These are intended to help you frame your thinking on creating the framework to build, distribute, and support your product so that it is profitable.

If you have more technical *How to* questions, they may be answered in the Force.com technical documentation or in Dummies books.

**Chapter**

# Questions for suits

*If I had eight hours to chop down a tree, I'd spend six hours sharpening my ax.*

**Abraham Lincoln (United States President, 1809 - 1865)**

BEFORE you start questioning whether the application can be developed in Force.com you need to figure out if you will survive a move to the Cloud. The worst thing you can do is spend a year's worth of time and money and then dump the entire effort.

First, there are some basic questions to help you figure out if this is worth pursuing for your business. What are the real drivers behind your desire to develop a Cloud based app? Are you being forced into it by customers or by competitors? If so, are they unwittingly pushing you into a far less profitable business, where the transition costs from your on-premise business will kill you? Or is the Cloud inevitable and you are feeling the need to move now to stay ahead of the curve?

Then, there are questions to help you prepare for a service-oriented business model. Have you understood all the costs involved? Do you understand the implications of running a business that's dependent on salesforce.com's strategy & platform? What do you need to do to drive the drastic change required within your organization?

## 6.1 Is Cloud Computing for me?

As we have seen the Cloud is a radical shift from the traditional on premise applications. There are a number of great advantages to moving to the Cloud, but there are a number of disadvantages as well. Effective preparation will involve figuring out how to manage your risk. These questions are the high-level commercially oriented questions you need to start asking.

| ☒ | Question | Why this matters |
|---|----------|------------------|
| ☐ | 6.1.1 Do you understand what will be different in the Cloud model? | We have talked about this before. The Cloud model is not about selling a product – it is a mechanism to help you provide a service. Most ISVs, such as the ones in Cases 1, 2, 6, 7 in Chapter 1 did not realize this. Business customers demand much higher service levels from a Cloud offering which drives up the costs significantly. Before jumping in, you must understand the most significant aspects to service delivery that you will be forced to deal with. This will not be a matter of your choice. You may just decide that this isn't the right model for you. Or you may decide that it isn't worth pursuing at this time since you have other critical things on your plate. |
| ☐ | 6.1.2 Have you lost business because you did not have a Cloud offering? | There is no more compelling reason to consider alternative approaches than when you are actively losing business. There is always the option to provide a solid defensive position with your customers based on your trusted relationship. You can explain the reasons why the Cloud may not be the right place for your sector just yet (security, data location, geo-redundancy, legislation). However, if cost is becoming a big issue for your prospects, this is something you may not be able to avoid. |

| ☒ | Question | Why this matters |
|---|----------|------------------|
| ☐ | 6.1.3 Is there pressure from your customers to move to Cloud Computing? | Even if you have not yet lost business directly, a sure sign of things to come is when your customers are talking and asking about your Cloud strategy. Even if you know that the Cloud is not right for your customers yet, you can be sure that someone else will go to them with a Cloud offering, and you need to be ready for that. |
| ☐ | 6.1.4 Are your existing competitors offering a Cloud solution? | Just as you are now thinking about the Cloud, it is likely that your competitors are as well and you need to be positioned to respond. Either with your own offering, or with a positive on-premise story. |
| ☐ | 6.1.5 Are new ISVs entering your market with a Cloud offering? | One of the reasons for considering the Cloud is that it provides the opportunity to extend your reach either geographically, or into other verticals. Unfortunately, just as this is good for you, it also means that other ISVs can extend into your markets. One of the challenges here is that you may not even be aware that these ISVs exist; never mind that they are competitors. |
| ☐ | 6.1.6 Are the industry analysts for your sector predicting that now is the right time for the Cloud? | Arguably, the first safe time to start your move to the Cloud is when the analysts for your sector start predicting the arrival of the Cloud. Although you will have missed the early adopter position you will have the benefit of not having spent as much time educating your customers. As always, there is a fine balance, and each business will have its own specificities that will determine where this balance point lies. |

| ☒ | Question | Why this matters |
|---|----------|------------------|
| ☐ | 6.1.7 Can you increase the barrier to entry for potential competitors? | If the application you want to deliver has little technical or business complexity, then this applies to your competitors as well as you. Can you create patents that lock out or make it difficult for your competitors or new entrants to follow you? Can you build exclusive partnerships with other vendors that may make it harder for others to match your value proposition? |
| ☐ | 6.1.8 Will it give you competitive advantage? | Being seen as offering a Cloud service may, in itself, enhance the market's perception of you. Any change is an opportunity to create differentiation and establish advantage in the market. You do need to think about whether you will be providing something that would be impossible if you didn't do it in the Cloud. Also, if your move to the Cloud is for defensive reasons, you need to determine if it is, in any way, diluting your current value proposition. |
| ☐ | 6.1.9 Are you perceived as safe, and want to add a little edge to your offerings? | Although the marketing noise is always about the latest and greatest thing, the reality is that most businesses are run on last year's technologies. Most companies are conservative by nature, and hence you may have established a great reputation as the safe trusted advisor. Adding the Cloud may add an edge to your offering. Have you thought about whether this is based, first and foremost, on offering value to your customers in the safe way they expect? |

| ☒ | Question | Why this matters |
|---|----------|------------------|
| ☐ | 6.1.10 Are you in a desperate place and need to do something radical? | This is a tough place to be. However, provided your investors and staff are clear about the risks and costs involved, it may be a great way to reinvent the business. The key is not to throw out all of your business experience. There are still real customers who need offerings to real issues and there needs to be a sound business plan. |
| ☐ | 6.1.11 Can you address new markets? | With the reach of the internet can you offer your solutions to geographies outside your home base? Although many of the traditional barriers to entry may be reduced, you may still need to consider partnering with local companies to provide local sales support, training or on-site consulting where required. |
| ☐ | 6.1.12 Can you address new industry verticals? | Due to the penetration of Salesforce CRM, Force.com may open up the opportunity to service additional verticals. Can you work with a larger customer base, across related industry verticals, by offering multiple variants on your core product? Is your company equipped to cope with servicing these new verticals? Will the additional costs be justified? Have you thought through all the organizational implications? Will these variations be better handled through partners? |

| ☒ | Question | Why this matters |
|---|---|---|
| ☐ | 6.1.13 Do you need to make your solution more responsive to change? | One of the challenges with the traditional on-premise software model is that it typically works on an annual product lifecycle. This would be fine if your code had no bugs and your market sector did not change from one year to the next. However, for many businesses, this is not the case. While bugs can be addressed through service patches, it may not be as simple to change business processes within a fast moving market sector. The centrally managed nature of a Cloud offering and the frequent release cycle makes it easier to make a change, and for it to be available to all customers. |
| ☐ | 6.1.14 Can you shorten sales cycles? | If you remove the need to install your software and you are able to demonstrate the production systems capability directly to the business line budget holder, without the need for IT department involvement, can you reduce the time to value for the customer, and shorten the sales cycle? |
| ☐ | 6.1.15 Will the Cloud make it easier for your customers to purchase? | If you have flexible payment terms, for example, monthly billing rather than a large upfront fee, then the budget holder may have authority to sign off on the costs directly. Also being able to OpEx the costs with clear options to cease payment may reduce the concerns about lock in and budget constraints. However, remember that for some businesses CapEx is still their preferred budgeting approach. So make sure you can still accept upfront cash! |

| ☒ | Question | Why this matters |
|---|----------|------------------|
| ☐ | 6.1.16  Can you reduce barriers to entry for new customers? | For new customers, your mature product or pricing models may just be too complex. Can you offer a diluted version through the Cloud, to provide a taste of the minimum functionality?  You may consider offering this at a significantly reduced price. |
| ☐ | 6.1.17  Can you improve time to market? | As with other items listed above, the Cloud provides the opportunity to introduce new ideas and functionality to all customers at a much faster rate than the traditional on-premise model.  Can you take advantage of this to bring new innovative ideas to market or to rapidly meet new legislative needs? |
| ☐ | 6.1.18  Do you need to add new capability to your product? | This could either be the driver for a complete rewrite, or a strategic approach to add new capability via the Cloud (where possible) to enhance the existing on premise offering. |
| ☐ | 6.1.19  Are your investors open to the idea of Cloud Computing? | Developing a Force.com application, which has enough IP to be valuable in the market, will probably require a level of investment that will be significant enough for your investors to care. Most investors today are well aware of the Cloud's potential and may be enthusiastic about the idea. However, they may still not see your business as a viable one in the Cloud. How much coaching and education do they need on the Cloud and your ability to support your business in the new model? |

| ☒ | Question | Why this matters |
|---|----------|------------------|
| ☐ | 6.1.20 How long have you existed as an on premise vendor? | Typically, the longer you've existed as an on-premise software vendor, the harder it will be to switch to the Cloud. You will need significant changes in every function of your organization, before you can really make a dent with your Cloud offering. You will also face fierce opposition from marketing, sales, product, and support functions. You will need to plan ahead for this contingency and figure out ways to mitigate your risks. |
| ☐ | 6.1.21 Do you already have a Cloud service that you offer? | Vendors that created SaaS products 4-5 years ago, before a PaaS was available, were true pioneers. Since you had to create your own infrastructure, scalability may become an issue as your business grows. The high cost of replicating and maintaining instances for each single tenant (or customer) may eventually catch up with you. Your margins may get lower as each new customer sucks up more resources. You may have to consider Force.com, and think of creating a true multi-tenant model that may help manage your costs better as your business scales. |
| ☐ | 6.1.22 Can you implement and sustain annuity payments from your customers? | Although it is theoretically possible to deliver Cloud-based applications using a perpetual license and software assurance it will be difficult. The customer expectation will be an annuity payment. It does not have to be monthly. Certainly corporations are happy to pay upfront, quarterly, or even annually. Many ISV business models are based on large, up-front payments to swiftly pay off development costs. If your model relies on this, the Cloud may not be appropriate. |

| ☒ | Question | Why this matters |
|---|----------|------------------|
| ☐ | 6.1.23 Have you considered buying a Cloud company? | They say that Cloud companies have a different DNA. It isn't just a matter of hiring a Force.com architect - the transformation required to get to that point will be huge. Depending on your size and other factors, you will have to figure out the kind of team that can get you there. Acquiring a successful Cloud company, that makes strategic sense, may also be a good way to force the change in your organization faster. |

## 6.2 Is Force.com the right Cloud Computing platform?

If you've decided that Cloud Computing is the right route forward you need to decide if Force.com should be your platform of choice. It is an important decision and there are a number of critical considerations. Once you start down this route, your success will be tied to salesforce.com and Force.com's success.

Evaluating Force.com as a development platform isn't the intent of this book – our goal is to help you figure out if it can help you build a successful Cloud Computing business.

Like most development platforms, Force.com provides a programming language, framework, APIs and services required to build a commercial app. Technology pundits may have varying opinions on how these features compare to other platforms.

Force.com also provides the ability to package and distribute your product in a multi-tenant model – a feature critical for commercial success in the Cloud. In addition to technical considerations, there may be important business considerations that may lead you to salesforce.com's platform.

This section will help you think through some of those.

| ☒ | Question | Why this matters |
|---|----------|------------------|
| ☐ | 6.2.1　Is there a clear overlap between your customers and salesforce.com's? | If you want to target customers of salesforce.com, building on Force.com is a very attractive proposition for you. You may have to put some effort into understanding your customers, your targets, as well as the salesforce.com installed base. The more synergies you can find, the stronger the imperative to build on Force.com. |
| ☐ | 6.2.2　Have you worked with salesforce.com before? | You may have had experience working with the Force.com platform and the core functionality of Salesforce CRM either as a customer or developer. Have you ever interacted with salesforce.com as a partner? Even more importantly, do you know anyone who has worked for a salesforce.com reseller? You need to understand what experience a reseller has had with salesforce.com in terms of marketing & sales help, support SLAs, accounting and ease of doing business. |
| ☐ | 6.2.3　Are you happy using a platform which is relatively new? | Force.com is relatively new to the market. Some companies are happy to trade feature rich environments and platforms for some degree of uncertainty related to longer term outlook. Others may prefer something better established and play it safe. You need to decide which camp you belong to. |

| ☒ | Question | Why this matters |
|---|----------|------------------|
| ☐ | 6.2.4   Are you happy being 'locked-in' to salesforce.com? | Make no mistake. If you start developing using Force.com you are locked into salesforce.com and their long term success. Even though salesforce.com has strategic alliances with Google, Amazon and Facebook, the fact remains that your app will be developed on a proprietary platform and language, as of today.  We must add that salesforce.com and VMware have recently partnered and announced VMforce – once available; VMforce will allow you to code your app in Java and run it in Salesforce.com's Cloud. However, we will have a better understanding of the pros and cons of coding in Java vs. Apex, only after VMforce is launched and tested. |
| ☐ | 6.2.5   What level of control do you need? | Using Force.com has many advantages. It removes much of the low-level plumbing and maintenance involved in delivering applications. It does this at the cost of some level of control. This may mean your application may not do exactly what you want, either in terms of user experience, programming logic, or performance. That the platform delivers functionality suitable for 99% of scenarios may be irrelevant if your competitive advantage is in the 1%. You need to appreciate this before you embark on using Force.com. |

| ☒ | Question | Why this matters |
|---|---|---|
| ☐ | 6.2.6 Have you created a set of criteria for your platform selection? | Most software vendors have a checklist that's really a list of features and functions of the desired product they want to build. Do you have a broader list that includes your projected financial numbers, fit with the salesforce.com culture, multi-tenancy requirements and how your target customers align with the salesforce.com customer base? |
| ☐ | 6.2.7 Why is multi-tenancy so important? | Force.com provides an opportunity for your own product to be multi-tenant. Why is this critical? Because you want a single code base of your product to serve all of your customers. If you don't do that, you will be spending way too much time and money managing each of your customers. Remember, controlling your costs is very critical in the Cloud model, since your customers will be paying you much less each year as compared to your on premise customers. |
| ☐ | 6.2.8 Do you need to store large quantities of data in salesforce.com's cloud? | There are limitations to the amount of storage that your customer will get with their Force.com licenses. More can be purchased but at a cost. There may also be some third-party data storage options that you can look into. Are there performance implications moving high volumes of data around, bearing in mind the location of salesforce.com or other third-party servers? |

| ☒ | Question | Why this matters |
|---|---|---|
| ☐ | 6.2.9 How do Force.com prices compare to those from other vendors? | This question completely depends what parts of Force.com you will be using, and the licenses you are going to use. Is your application dependent on using the CRM capability? What are the typical user profiles? How do the prices for each of these license types stack up against other vendor approaches? |
| ☐ | 6.2.10 Do you want to own the billing relationship with your customers? | You will obviously need to bill your customers on a monthly, quarterly, six-monthly or an annual basis. Billing and all the infrastructure around it is a significant overhead. You need to decide if you have the capacity internally to do it. |
| ☐ | 6.2.11 Do you want to resell salesforce.com product licenses? | Being a reseller of salesforce.com implies that you will also have to resell their licenses as part of your product. In that case, you will have to sell a bundle containing your product and Force.com seats, and then pay salesforce.com on a monthly basis. If you're not comfortable with that model, you'll have to figure out how to sell your product as a plug-in and have salesforce.com sell their seats directly. |
| ☐ | 6.2.12 Will salesforce.com gain new customers because of your app? | Salesforce.com will love you if your product helps them increase their seat sales. Ideally, if every user of your product has to buy a Force.com seat as well, they will be more invested in your success. Does your app offer that ability? How would this impact your revenue model? |

| ☒ | Question | Why this matters |
|---|----------|------------------|
| ☐ | 6.2.13 Does your application require customers to already have, or be prepared to implement Salesforce CRM? | Salesforce.com offers several products, depending on customer or partner needs. As a reseller or an OEM partner, you can only resell the platform products from salesforce.com and not their CRM products. You need to figure out if your application is dependent on features such as Campaigns or Opportunities that are only provided by the CRM product (since you may not be allowed to resell the CRM product, it may change your strategy). It will impact your go-to-market as well as product pricing. |
| ☐ | 6.2.14 What if integrations may be required with customer's existing systems? | Any Cloud based solution will have some challenges when tightly integrating with a customer's on-premise systems. However, the APIs provided by Force.com may facilitate integration with customer apps, without losing your ability to provide upgrades to them. Will you be bundling this integration within your product or will you have to handle integration separately for each customer? |
| ☐ | 6.2.15 Is salesforce.com your largest competitor? | Is your app on their roadmap? If you've seen an opportunity, then why wouldn't they? Typically, if you're targeting a smaller, niche market segment with very deep functionality, chances are that salesforce.com won't get in your way. On the other hand, if you're planning to offer something that may become commoditized, or if you're planning to offer a very specialized feature that is an extension of CRM, it may eventually find its way on the salesforce.com roadmap. |

| ☒ | Question | Why this matters |
|---|----------|------------------|
| ☐ | 6.2.16 How defensible is your IP? | If you can build the application using Force.com, how quickly can your competitors? And does that matter? |
| ☐ | 6.2.17 Do you know how you will handle competition from the salesforce.com sales teams? | Building on Force.com doesn't mean everyone at salesforce.com will be in your camp. Their direct selling team may become your biggest competitor if your offering is perceived to impinge on products sold by them. You will have to determine if it's worth increasing your competition by building on their platform. |
| ☐ | 6.2.18 Is there competition from other salesforce.com partners? | You need to check if there are other salesforce.com partners that already offer your application, or a lighter version of it, in some form. Long term salesforce.com partners may have significant experience as well as support from salesforce.com corporate team and may prove to be tough competitors for you. You will need a plan to mitigate that risk. |
| ☐ | 6.2.19 Can you benefit from salesforce.com's marketing? | Salesforce.com has one of the best marketing teams that the technology world has seen. There are several ways that you can use the salesforce.com marketing to your advantage and save some marketing dollars. However, for certain products it may be better to market your product independently or in alignment with other vendors that are dominant in your industry or business area. This decision will impact your overall marketing strategy and costs. |

| ☒ | Question | Why this matters |
|---|----------|------------------|
| ☐ | 6.2.20 Do you think your current or future customers visit the AppExchange? | ISVs sometimes assume that their prospects will download their apps through the AppExchange at the same rate that consumers download music on iTunes. In reality, business buyers are harder to reach and take forever to convince. In addition, certain types of customers may not even visit the AppExchange. Re there other places where your customers may find you? |
| ☐ | 6.2.21 Will the salesforce.com offering enhance your product? | Certain standard features provided by Force.com may significantly enhance your product's value to your customer. For instance, the in-built reporting capability may be extremely useful and may eliminate the need for you to build your own reporting function, if reporting is important to your customers. Chatter is another example of a recently released in-built feature that may be very useful if your customers value conversations/collaboration within their enterprise. |
| ☐ | 6.2.22 Can salesforce.com own the relationship if Salesforce functionality is greater than your product? | In certain situations your customers, after buying your product, may get attracted to other features offered by Salesforce CRM that aren't included in the bundled Force.com seats provided by you. In that situation, salesforce.com will want to establish a direct relationship with your customer. Are you comfortable with that scenario? |

| ☒ | Question | Why this matters |
|---|----------|------------------|
| ☐ | 6.2.23 When it's time to renew, who would reach out to customers first – you or salesforce.com? | Since your Cloud product will run on the Force.com platform, your customers will also be salesforce.com customers. Salesforce.com direct sales reps may also reach out to your customers, creating a competitive situation. You will need to figure out how to mitigate that risk. |
| ☐ | 6.2.24 Is Force.com secure? | The question is not "Is it Secure" but "Is it secure enough for your customers." Will you be able to make your customers comfortable? |
| ☐ | 6.2.25 Will your customers have a large number of *their* customers accessing the app through the internet? | Your customers may have a need for *their* customers to access the app. That would mean building a capability for their customers to access the app without a full product license. Force.com provides robust Sites and Customer Portal capabilities to facilitate that and it could work out to be a significant cost advantage. |
| ☐ | 6.2.26 Do you need to provide content management capabilities to your customers? | Force.com offers basic content management which is fully integrated with the platform. If your customers have internal or external users that need to access content, this capability can be really useful depending on the level of sophistication you need. |

| ☒ | Question | Why this matters |
|---|----------|------------------|
| ☐ | 6.2.27 Can Force.com cope with your processing needs? | Even though it is a very robust platform, Force.com may or may not work for you, depending on certain processing speeds required by your app or transaction processing capabilities that you may need. In addition, there are various governor limits that are imposed, which you may need to work around. Sometimes, they may pose a real hindrance and may add to the cost/effort. You may have to look into the published list of limits, to ascertain what workarounds you will need. |
| ☐ | 6.2.28 Where is the data stored? | In many countries around the world there are strict controls on where data is allowed to be physically stored. This is a special concern with Government data. You need to ensure Force.com has a datacenter in an appropriate geographic region to allay these concerns. |
| ☐ | 6.2.29 How is the data backed up? | With traditional on-premise applications you can back up all of your data on to storage devices. You can touch it and see it. Customers take a lot of comfort from this. Although data is triple-stored in Force.com across different "fault-zones" and is theoretically impossible to lose, you need to determine the comfort level of your customers with this idea. |
| ☐ | 6.2.30 What is your Service Level Agreement? | By using Force.com you are committing to their Service Level Agreements (SLA). Are these SLAs sufficient for your customer? Are the remedies for breach of the SLA in line with the remedies demanded of you by your customer? |

| ☒ | Question | Why this matters |
|---|----------|------------------|
| ☐ | 6.2.31 What is salesforce.com's track record against its SLAs and agreements with other partners and resellers? | Companies have varying needs. There are several areas where you will be very dependent on salesforce.com. For instance, support is one area where you will frequently need salesforce.com engineers to troubleshoot certain aspects of your service that are out of your control. You may want to get some basic benchmarks as well as check with other salesforce.com resellers regarding their experience with such support. |
| ☐ | 6.2.32 Will salesforce.com support you when you go for funding? | If you will be looking for outside funding, at some point, for your new product or for your entire company, VCs will want to know how supportive salesforce.com is of your product and how they will help you succeed, since you will be dependent on their platform. |
| ☐ | 6.2.33 What is the long-term future of salesforce.com? | Force.com may become the PaaS of choice for the entire world. Salesforce.com may turn into a tech giant like Google. On the other hand, salesforce.com may be acquired by a larger company with a competing offering and Force.com may be discontinued. All of them are possible scenarios. Since you will be tied to their success, this is an important consideration for you. |

## 6.3 Commercial Considerations

Cloud Computing and Force.com open up a number of new business models. Any change of business model can have profound implications on the organization, motivation and compensation of both your front and back office operations.

The move to Cloud Computing also has implications on the metrics you use to judge the health and wellbeing of your company and the way you manage the finances.

With the potential for dramatically different cash flows and profit margins, getting investment for the company and managing the investor's expectations may need to be approached differently.

This is probably the most critical area for you to consider, hence there are more questions in this section than any other.

| ☒ | Question | Why this matters |
|---|----------|------------------|
| ☐ | 6.3.1 What is the cost of doing nothing? | Is doing nothing an acceptable situation and if so what would this cost you? You might be trying to protect an existing product, customer base or market position that may not actually justify the costs. Although a tough call, it may be better to accept the costs of getting out now and not pouring more good money after bad. Better to ask this question now than $500k down the road. |
| ☐ | 6.3.2 Will there be revenue loss during transition? | If customers know that you are bringing a new offering to market will they delay purchasing decisions? Can you estimate this drop in revenue and, more importantly, can you survive it? |
| ☐ | 6.3.3 What level of cannibalization? | There will be some customers who may want to move to the Force.com service from your on-premise model for a range of reasons. This will definitely hit your short term revenue. Have you estimated the hit correctly? |
| ☐ | 6.3.4 How much will it cost to develop the app? | This is not necessarily the cost of developing and implementing a module of your app for one customer. The 2nd, 3rd, 4th and ... customers will all suck up the same cost if you don't spend time upfront to "productize" your app. You must calculate the minimum cost to develop the first version of a multi-tenant 'product', not a single-tenant app. |

| ☒ | Question | Why this matters |
|---|----------|------------------|
| ☐ | 6.3.5 What is the cost to create subsequent versions? | In the Cloud and the salesforce.com world, customers are used to getting free upgrades seamlessly. When you go back to your customers with upgrades, they will not like added costs or interruptions, particularly when salesforce.com will be giving them free upgrades of the Force.com platform every 3 months with no disruption. Upgrades may also include bug fixes in the form of patches or releases. You will also need a very strong versioning strategy. All this comes at a cost. In addition, there will be a cost to develop the new functionality. |
| ☐ | 6.3.6 How much will the Force.com licenses cost? | You need to be clear what type of Force.com and Salesforce licenses may be required for customers. How can you minimize these costs? If it is worth it to them, salesforce.com may be open to creative licensing. |
| ☐ | 6.3.7 What are the marketing costs for rebranding/ positioning? | You will need to invest in a marketing & communications program, which is covered in the next section. This will cover not only your prospects and customers, but also your partners, industry watchers, your own staff and other stakeholders. |
| ☐ | 6.3.8 What are the costs to provide support? | You may now be offering your products on a global basis, but does this require investment in a multilingual, 24 x 7 help desk? Your support team may become your primary contact point with customers. For example, some customers may sign up online with little face to face direct sales interaction and this may require stronger help desk skills and training. |

| ☒ | Question | Why this matters |
|---|----------|------------------|
| ☐ | 6.3.9 How will implementation services change? | Your product is already installed so the amount of infrastructure installation services is likely to be reduced. Is this a core part of your profitable revenue or is it a loss leader that you may be glad to get rid of? Will customers expect to live with less training and implementation support putting your projects at risk? Just because the service is in the Cloud, the time to implement inside a customer's business may not change, so you may have to think about how to deal with that cost. |
| ☐ | 6.3.10 Are additional professional services critical to your commercial model? | For many organizations the professional services that they offer around their products are the high margin elements at the heart of their commercial model – services such as customization, business process change, integration and migration services, local onsite customer support etc. Will customers of your Cloud service be willing to pay for all these services? Will any of these services impact your ability to keep your product multi-tenant? Will you be able to offer these services in a different type of package? |
| ☐ | 6.3.11 How will the new offering affect your sales costs? | This is not just about costs associated with retraining existing sales staff. You need to consider the new costs of sales such as online sign up, automated provisioning tools, credit/debit card payment etc. |

| ☒ | Question | Why this matters |
|---|----------|------------------|
| ☐ | 6.3.12 How will you handle micro billing? | If you currently have a few hundred customers with one invoice per year, how will your costs change if you have thousands of customers with invoices every month? The cost of invoicing can quickly become a significant percentage of the overall costs. |
| ☐ | 6.3.13 How will you handle salesforce.com invoices? | You will have to deal with salesforce.com sending you separate invoices for each customer, every month since they will be charging you for the Force.com component of your sale. As your customer base grows, handling an invoice per customer every month can become a huge overhead. |
| ☐ | 6.3.14 Are there any 3$^{rd}$ party or partner costs to consider? | There may be other 3$^{rd}$ parties who you decide to work with, either to accelerate deployment (services partners) or for sales and marketing. Will there be costs involved in integrating products or services or in managing multiple contracts? |
| ☐ | 6.3.15 Do you have a sense of what a customer will pay, by segment or market? | If you were hoping to get $1000 per user per month for your Cloud service, you are in for a disappointment. For most Cloud products today, with some exceptions, irrespective of industry or functional area, customers pay from $5 to $200 per user per month. The price may also vary by geographical area. For instance, Navatar Group's Capital Markets app for Force.com fetches $125 per user per month in North America but is priced at $75 in India. You will need to figure out the market price that your product will command, to put together a solid business case. |

| ☒ | Question | Why this matters |
|---|----------|------------------|
| ☐ | 6.3.16  Who will be the party that pays for your offering? | This may seem an odd question. However it possible that a 3$^{rd}$ party chooses to pay on behalf of the ultimate user because they would get huge benefits. An example of this is the Zanzibar eProcurement project where the Government buying departments pay for the supplier portal so that all suppliers can interact electronically with the Government for free. Having a 3$^{rd}$ party as your customer provides you a ready sales channel in addition to other potential benefits such as the costs of sales and administration. It may also be effective in managing churn. |
| ☐ | 6.3.17  Does your offering need to generate revenue directly or indirectly? | Where are you going to earn your money? Is this offering intended to fully recover costs through direct product sales or is it a proxy for other services such as support, consulting and training or as a light offering to encourage customers to your premium offering. Be aware that if it is a proxy or a light offering you will most probably not be building a Cloud product but a services business. |
| ☐ | 6.3.18  Are you going to generate revenue from ad funding? | There has been a lot of noise about offering software for free and then generating revenue through advertising. Google is the obvious answer for this.  A note of warning; the revenue models only really work for very high volume services. In addition, someone will also have to pay for the Force.com license costs. |

| ☒ | Question | Why this matters |
|---|----------|------------------|
| ☐ | 6.3.19 Will you be charging based on named users or usage? | Most Cloud companies charge their customers based on named users, on a monthly basis. However, there may be other ways to charge your customers based on their size, revenue, product usage, etc. You may need to negotiate a corresponding agreement with salesforce.com for buying Force.com seats and see if a different pricing model will work for you. |
| ☐ | 6.3.20 What is the charge period for your service? | If you do have recurring fees, do you charge for these on a monthly, quarterly or even annual basis? This has a huge impact on the cost of back office administration and cash flow. In addition, your customer's ability to pay may also be a factor. Be aware, that you will have to pay salesforce.com for seats, on a monthly basis. |
| ☐ | 6.3.21 Will you offer 'pay ahead' discounts? | Despite the benefits of an annuity revenue stream there is nothing like cash in the bank. So you may offer a discount for customers who will pay for a year (or two) in advance. For example, pay for 11 months, get the 12th free. |
| ☐ | 6.3.22 Will you offer special incentives for your initial customers? | Navatar Group offers discounted pricing for their Force.com-based offering for financial firms, during the first year. Will you be able to sustain a similar incentive plan to get a jump start on building your customer base? |

| ☒ | Question | Why this matters |
|---|----------|------------------|
| ☐ | 6.3.23  Are you going to enforce minimum contract terms? | Salesforce.com will most probably require you to sign 12 month contracts with your customers. If you think your customers will not be willing to commit to yearly contracts, how will you manage this? |
| ☐ | 6.3.24  Do you need to include variable usage charges? | If a customer's use of the service increases your overheads (or what you will need to pay salesforce.com), then you need a way to recover these costs. This could be part of either a license or annuity model. You also need to consider whether your usage charges are truly reflecting usage (transaction charging) or are based some reasonable approximation (organizational size; the bigger you are, the more you are likely to consume). |
| ☐ | 6.3.25  Will you be offering a free trial period? | Free trials are very popular in the Cloud world. In fact, your customers will expect free 30 day trials of your service. The good news is that salesforce.com does allow you to offer free trials. However, trials can also extend your sales cycle and drive up your costs. In our experience, customers are not able to effectively evaluate complex apps without significant handholding during the trial period. Depending on your app and customer base, you may have to ascertain whether free trials will work with your financial model. |

| ☒ | Question | Why this matters |
|---|----------|------------------|
| ☐ | 6.3.26 Will you charge on-off setup fees? | There may be up-front costs involved for each customer, which you may want to recover from the outset. This could be a large chunk of services work or purchase of specific hardware or software. On the one hand this seems to go against the 'pay as you go' Cloud model. However it is perfectly acceptable in some sectors with complex integration and data migration needs. |
| ☐ | 6.3.27 Are differentiated support options a means to generate revenue? | You may wish to offer a basic support offering as part of your service. For example, email and self help, with limited response time guarantees. Where customers want a more rapid response, as well as more options to contact you, you may be able to impose a premium charge. |
| ☐ | 6.3.28 Are there any economies of scale across your delivery model? | Although costs will normally increase as you get more customers, you will also gain efficiencies and volume discounts that can reduce your cost per customer and hence increase your margin. How can you validate these types of assumptions for your business plan? |
| ☐ | 6.3.29 How does your pricing compare to your competitors? | Fantastic offering, great launch planning and aggressive pricing – until you see your nearest competitor is 50% cheaper. Understand why and react accordingly - lower margin expectations, limited infrastructure costs or lower cost of sales. Or maybe they can afford to lose money to drive you out of the market. It may also be quite possible that they have got their metrics wrong and cannot sustain their business. |

| ☒ | Question | Why this matters |
|---|----------|------------------|
| ☐ | 6.3.30 What assumptions have you made about user volumes? | The Cloud offers the chance to significantly extend your reach and hence have higher customer numbers. But what is reasonable? Be cautious of a top down approach that goes something like: There are 10 million potential customers. Surely we can get 5% of these - because 5% seems like a small number. Therefore we will have 500,000 customers. A better approach is to figure out how many customers you can realistically acquire and service in year one and year two, and then work upwards. |
| ☐ | 6.3.31 What assumptions have you made for take up velocity? | Companies who go from zero to millions of customers overnight make great headlines but are not normal. That said you do need to have a plan for growth, usually from the second year onwards, which is based on your own ability to acquire and service customers, as opposed to assuming they will all flock to you. |
| ☐ | 6.3.32 How will you handle bad debt and risk management? | As you get more customers, especially in remote locations with minimal personal relationships, it is likely that bad debt could increase. You need to provide for this and any processes you adopt to manage it, including deliberate fraudulent activity. |
| ☐ | 6.3.33 What metrics will you use to measure performance? | Depending on the models and GTM strategies you choose, you may need to review the metrics and KPIs used to monitor the health of the business. Examples could be a shift from new sales revenue to long term revenue retention targets and to velocity of sales rather than revenue value. |

| ☒ | Question | Why this matters |
|---|----------|------------------|
| ☐ | 6.3.34  Do you need to review your accounting procedures? | Does the way you recognize revenue have to alter the way you book costs?  How will sales bonuses be accounted for?  And if you are now working across multiple geographies there will be new rules and regulations that need to be considered?  Have you accounted for those? |
| ☐ | 6.3.35  Do you need to accept credit/debit card payments? | With high volume, low value services that are billed periodically, credit cards may be the right answer.  How does this work with your existing systems? |
| ☐ | 6.3.36  Are there tax breaks available to you? | Across the globe there are various tax breaks for businesses who are working in valued areas of technology, or who are entering new markets, or working with local companies. These can be valuable sources of funding especially during the early stages. |
| ☐ | 6.3.37  Do your partners offer any funding support? | One of your partners may have a strategic interest in your Cloud offering and may be interested in investing.  Funding may also come from a partner in the form of items that may have value to you but may not cost much to them. |

# 6.4 What is your Go-to-Market Strategy?

Driving demand in this new market will be critical. Although Cloud Computing may be perceived by many as synonymous with the low cost/free consumer oriented service with little or no support (basically clever websites) there is in reality a wide range of services available all the way up to global enterprise offerings. It is important that you are able to differentiate between them both internally and with your customers, and then set your pricing and value proposition accordingly.

Should you be using the book *Thinking of.. Buying Cloud Computing* book as marketing collateral to help educate your customers?

Will a more consultative approach be required, even though this seems to run counter to the high volume, low touch approach that the Cloud seems to be all about? This could result in longer sales cycles, smaller initial orders and require more experienced salespeople. But long term order value could be greater.

Your go to market may vary by size of company, industry vertical and geography. Are you clear about your target markets and the approach you are taking for each?

Can you piggy-back on salesforce.com's PR and marketing activities. Even more importantly, can you leverage their customer base to your advantage? But how do you make sure that you differentiate yourself from them?

Once you have a hot lead how are you going to service it; direct sales, resellers, partners, system integrators, online? How about all of the above? How will channel conflict with salesforce.com and your own resellers play out? How does your channel strategy fit with your existing go to market, if you have a current offering?

There will be several important considerations in this new world. Here are some critical questions for you to answer.

| ☒ | Question | Why this matters |
|---|----------|------------------|
| ☐ | 6.4.1 Which are your target markets? | Are you extending your existing markets or expanding into new ones? Are you moving into new geographies? Does the Cloud offering create opportunities in new sectors? Will you be able to target companies larger or smaller than your current customers? What is the overlap with salesforce.com's customer base? Can you upsell to salesforce.com's customers? Can salesforce.com upsell to your customers? There will be many such important questions to be answered, related to your target customers. |
| ☐ | 6.4.2 Can the salesforce.com marketing and PR be helpful? | Yes, but it can only be helpful if your own marketing is on target. Rather than waiting for the salesforce.com marketing team to help get your word out, you may have to figure out how to leverage the salesforce.com brand to your advantage. That's what most successful Force.com resellers do. Once you have the basics in place and get some early successes, the salesforce.com Marketing and PR teams will surely be influential allies. |
| ☐ | 6.4.3 What are the best mechanisms for generating leads? | There is no hard and fast rule. It really depends on your industry. Some industries, such as high-tech, respond well to promotional emails whereas others, such as manufacturing, rely more on solid industry credentials. You will need to create a strategy taking into account several factors such as your industry preferences, newer marketing channels, salesforce.com's marketing strategy, and your team's proficiency. |

| ☒ | Question | Why this matters |
|---|----------|------------------|
| ☐ | 6.4.4 How are you presenting yourself to the market? | Are you positioning yourself as bleeding edge, always looking for the newest ways to help customers? Or are you safe and slow, but have now decided that the Cloud is prime time and it is time to embrace it and help your trusted customers? How does this play with your current brand positioning? If you are trying to change your style (conservative to leading edge or vice versa) how will this affect how you can use your existing marketing capability? |
| ☐ | 6.4.5 Which customer segments will you target? | You're probably thinking you already know who you want to target. After all, you already have a successful on premise product. Most ISVs find, though, that their target market in the Cloud turns out to be different from what they originally had in mind. You may have to reassess your target segments upfront. |
| ☐ | 6.4.6 What segmentation are you using? | In static markets, segmentation often ends up as broad categorization. For example, organization size, number of PC's or seats etc. However, in more dynamic markets, you may wish to consider other segmentation. For example, in the current economic climate, issues such as cash poor vs. cash rich or OpEx vs. CapEx may talk to a demand for a Cloud service. Also the rate of growth geographically can indicate a need for Cloud services. In addition, don't forget to take a look at how salesforce.com is segmenting their customers. |

| ☒ | Question | Why this matters |
|---|----------|------------------|
| ☐ | 6.4.7 How does a PEST analysis affect your GTM? | This may be an established model for assessing the buying environment, but it still offers an insight into what is driving your customer's buying decisions (PEST stands for Political, Economic, Social and Technical). |
| ☐ | 6.4.8 How credible are you? | A challenge for any new offering is to convince potential customers that you are credible. Can you leverage your existing experience? Are your current case studies valid for the new offering? Do you have early adopters who you can reference? Do you have a track record of delivering new ideas successfully? Can you get credibility by association (for example, being showcased by a major partner such as salesforce.com, Amazon, Google)? |
| ☐ | 6.4.9 Have you considered Blue Ocean value differentiation? | This is an approach that looks to make your competition irrelevant by redefining the market opportunity. For example, the way Nintendo changed the gaming market with the Wiimote by opening up gaming to the casual, non skilled gamer by focusing on ease of use rather than high-cost graphics. |
| ☐ | 6.4.10 Can you learn from your direct competitors? | What are they doing? Are you leading or following? If they haven't moved, why not? Can you gain significant first mover advantage? If you are a follower, can you learn from their mistakes rather than simply duplicate their efforts? Can you leap frog them? |

| ☒ | Question | Why this matters |
|---|----------|------------------|
| ☐ | 6.4.11 Will salesforce.com be a competitor? | What confidence do you have that your product is not on salesforce.com's roadmap? If you see a business opportunity, why wouldn't they? Have you done enough research into whether the magnitude of the opportunity is attractive enough for salesforce.com to consider going after? |
| ☐ | 6.4.12 Can you learn from examples in other industries? | The high tech business world of IT often seems to believe that it is so far ahead of everyone else that there is nothing to learn from others. Consider this position and look at other industries. The insurance sector has for years worked on the basis of small long term referral revenue. Outsourcing non-core services is normal in many sectors so why should outsourcing IT be considered new? |
| ☐ | 6.4.13 Where are your potential customers talking? | Customers are increasingly using new media (blogs, online forums, communities and even Facebook or Twitter) to both self educate and comment about their business needs and experiences. By identifying this you may be able to target messaging to specific groups. |
| ☐ | 6.4.14 Can you control the conversation? | Brand protection and controlled messaging has been a key goal for most companies. However, in the online world this is often not possible. You may be able to control the messaging on your own web site, or on forums where you may be the moderator (although you may be risking your credibility). It may be harder to control social media discussions on Facebook and Twitter? |

| ☒ | Question | Why this matters |
|---|----------|------------------|
| ☐ | 6.4.15 What role will User Groups play? | User groups can be great for feedback and establishing yourself as credible about user engagement. However they can also create inertia by insisting that things do not change too much. Can you use an existing user group to identify early adopters for your offering? Can they help guide the business requirements? Can they provide promotion and credibility as you go to market? |
| ☐ | 6.4.16 What role will the AppExchange play? | Will your customers be looking on the AppExchange? How do you differentiate your application from others which are cheaper but inferior? How much effort do you put into getting good reviews and a high profile? Do you use your marketing to direct customers to the AppExchange or your own website? |
| ☐ | 6.4.17 Are your target buyers web-centric? | By understanding the style of your buying community you can correctly target your messaging. Do they use the web for research, online purchasing etc? Or do they prefer a human face with physical paper contracts? Offering an online, technology-focused messaging and signup campaign may not be the best idea, if your target customer is a traditionally minded 50 year old accountant! |

| ☒ | Question | Why this matters |
|---|----------|------------------|
| ☐ | 6.4.18 Should you consider niche marketing? | With a potentially huge audience available to you in the Cloud, it is important that your message is heard. The challenge is that a generic message may be applicable to all, but is of interest to none. By focusing on a niche you can ensure that you talk to their specific needs. Once you have gained success in one niche, you can approach a related niche that will value your previous experience. |
| ☐ | 6.4.19 Have you started a blog yet? | More and more buyers today are monitoring blogs to get a pulse on their customers and the industry. Does your company have a blog yet? Do you visit other related blogs and comment on them? Is there an opportunity for you to start a conversation with your potential customers through blogging? |
| ☐ | 6.4.20 Do you go to market direct, or through channels of influence? | Going direct gives you control. Channels of influence can extend your reach and provide credibility. Maybe a combination is right for you. In your home market where you have an established presence, you may go direct. For new sectors or overseas, linking with an established player as your channel may accelerate your growth. Going direct initially may be a good way of building collateral and case studies, which will be required to convince other channels to work with you. |

| ☒ | Question | Why this matters |
|---|----------|------------------|
| ☐ | 6.4.21 Will your plans create channel conflict with your existing partners? | If you go direct or introduce new partners, will this upset your existing partners? Does the pricing for your Cloud offering undercut your other offerings? If you are a start-up then these problems do not exist, but for established ISVs this needs to be considered. |
| ☐ | 6.4.22 Where will you get your initial case studies? | Most buyers are conservative and want somebody else to try an offering before they pay for it. Early adopter evidence can be critical to mass sales. Can you use your existing customer base? Do you offer advantageous pricing to the first group of customers - may be even give it away free. Is this built into your business model? |
| ☐ | 6.4.23 How do you accelerate time to value? | With on-premise solutions, the customer typically buys the offering from you and then finds a way to make it work. This can require significant effort and cost and, once completed, creates a barrier to churn. With online offerings there is typically little (perceived) upfront effort. If the user does not quickly get value from the service, there is no sunken investment that stops them from leaving. Time to value becomes a key metric. |
| ☐ | 6.4.24 How are you positioning the future for your existing offering(s)? | If you are offering a replacement to an existing offering, even if functionally weaker initially, how will you prioritize sales for your new vs. the current offering? Can the customer base be a target for new sales or is this a cash cow that needs to have its life extended? |

| ☒ | Question | Why this matters |
|---|----------|------------------|
| ☐ | 6.4.25 What will your pricing model be? | You have many choices, each with their own pros and cons. Free, as a lead to professional services and support revenue. Ad funded (be careful to fully understand the HUGE volumes required to make this viable). Freemium, where the few who need your professional offering cover the costs of the free to use service. Sponsored, where there is value in one party paying for the service so that others can have it for free. Or usage based. And none of this stops you having a very traditional pricing model based on seats! But remember to factor in what you will have to pay salesforce.com as well as the ability to add/drop seats. |
| ☐ | 6.4.26 Do you offer specific and focused landing pages on your web site? | How quick and easy is it for potential customers to get what they want when they arrive at your site. Do they need to have links to your company history and every product you sell? They have probably already done their research and this is distracting noise. If they are here to buy, then a dedicated landing page with specific calls to action could significantly increase closure rates. |

| ☒ | Question | Why this matters |
|---|----------|------------------|
| ☐ | 6.4.27  Do you offer 'Try before you buy'? | Free trials are very popular in the Cloud world. In fact, your customers will expect free 30 day trials of your service. The good news is that salesforce.com does allow you to offer free trials. Will a user be any more likely to buy if you offer them 6 months free, rather than 1 month?  Asking for credit card details so you can automatically start charging at the end of the free period may also be an option, if it doesn't put your customers off. However, trials can also extend your sales cycle and drive up your costs. In our experience, customers are not able to effectively evaluate complex apps without significant handholding during the trial period. Depending on your app and customer base, you may have to ascertain whether free trials will work for you. |
| ☐ | 6.4.28  Will using online ad words be part of your marketing mix? | This is a subject in its own right and can be hugely successful or a massive waste of time, effort and money. |
| ☐ | 6.4.29  Will you need a new sales team for the Force.com service? | You probably have salespeople already that are good at selling your on premise service. Will the same sales team suffice or will you need fresh talent? Can your sales team sell salesforce.com features as well? Can they sell to smaller companies or firms that need fewer seats, since that sale may be quite different? |

| ☒ | Question | Why this matters |
|---|----------|------------------|
| ☐ | 6.4.30  Can the sales process be mostly remote? | A big advantage of Cloud products is that potential customers are comfortable with the idea of remote demos through web-conferencing and other tools. This can really reduce the cost of sales. Can you switch to this model since some of your competitors in the Cloud may already be thinking about it? |

## 6.5 Migrating to the Cloud and Force.com

If you are a new start-up you may feel that you can skip these questions. But don't. There may be questions that you will find useful and insightful as your business matures.

If you have an established business, then this is where the really hard decisions start.

With any new idea the first thing that happens is that the supporters take a position as far away from the existing model. In the case of Cloud Computing this means taking the model of on-premise software with perpetual licensing and turning it into hosted software with rental or annuity licensing.

Whilst this is potentially great for start-ups, it is not so straightforward for established players. There could be a potentially large investment and may require a leap of faith to make this major shift. Which is probably why so many ISVs have held a watching brief.

However, the market is maturing and customer's expectations are increasing. So as always we are heading towards a hybrid world where businesses need their operations to be joined up and available whether they are on-line or off-line. This opens the door for existing ISVs to leverage their greater maturity and enter the game - provided they can quickly learn the new rules.

| ☒ | Question | Why this matters |
|---|----------|------------------|
| ☐ | 6.5.1 Is Cloud Computing a new product stream? | Is your Cloud solution offering new functionality not currently in your existing products? Will your existing products be able to call this new capability to enhance their existing capability or will it be sold independently? If the latter is not your preferred plan it will be harder for you to pull this off. |
| ☐ | 6.5.2 Is Cloud Computing a parallel offering? | Are you building a parallel offering with essentially the same capabilities but delivered through the Cloud? If that is the case you may be setting yourself up for failure. For your Cloud product to succeed, it will have a very different set of features, value proposition and customer segments. You may have to rethink this. |
| ☐ | 6.5.3 Is the migration an evolution or a revolution? | Several companies have tried using their existing apps, infrastructure and people to introduce a Cloud offering – this evolution approach has seldom worked. The Cloud requires a fundamentally different business model, architecture and mindset and needs to be approached as a revolution, if you are really serious. Are you ready to take that risk? |

| ☒ | Question | Why this matters |
|---|---|---|
| ☐ | 6.5.4 Can you afford to run separate businesses? | One of the challenges when offering two similar offerings is that you can create sales conflict between your products and, therefore, within your sales teams. One option is to establish a new business and brand to market and sell the Cloud offering. Although this has merits there is also the overhead of running two businesses/brands and the risk of potential dilution of the original business brand. It may of course be part of the business plan to migrate to a new brand. The key is to be clear about what the costs, benefits and risks are. |
| ☐ | 6.5.5 What commitments to existing customers do you have? | Before you leap into the Cloud and bring your existing customers with you, have you thought about what commitments, especially contractual, may be inconsistent with the Cloud? Some of the key areas to check are security, data location and protection, and legal responsibilities. |
| ☐ | 6.5.6 What are the internal barriers to migration? | Are there potential barriers to migration? These include staff departing, limited resources (people and money), lack of support from key people within the business, sales staff motivated to sell the existing offering over the new Cloud one. How seriously should you take these barriers? |
| ☐ | 6.5.7 What are the external milestones for the migration? | Are there compelling deadlines that provide milestones to aim for? These will not only provide drivers internally, but also create compelling events that may make customers consider your new offering. For example, are there legislative changes or key changes in your sector? |

| ☒ | Question | Why this matters |
|---|----------|------------------|
| ☐ | 6.5.8 What are the external barriers to migration? | The external barriers may be a frustration that prevents you and your customers realizing the Cloud dream or they could be the basis for you to decide the timing. You may want to establish your position with customers as a safe pair of hands. Things to consider are legal, regulatory, marketplace conditions and availability (especially geo location). Sometimes, a barrier may be something as basic as lack of reliable internet access. |
| ☐ | 6.5.9 Is your entire organization excited about the Cloud? | In most cases, it may seem that everyone is excited about the Cloud, but if you dig deeper you may find it's just a curiosity more than anything else. It may help tremendously to figure out the reasons, if any, for which various people that matter in your organization will commit to this effort. You will need to sell this internally first. |
| ☐ | 6.5.10 Do you know what you will migrate to Force.com? | Some people approach this with a firm resolve to migrate a certain app, say Contract Management, to the Cloud. Others know they need to rebuild one of their apps in the Cloud, to test the water, but aren't sure which one. The reality is that your initial hypothesis may turn out to be very different from what you end up doing because of customer expectations in the Cloud that you may not yet be aware of. |

| ☒ | Question | Why this matters |
|---|----------|------------------|
| ☐ | 6.5.11 Have you defined the requirements? | It's great if you have. However, it's important to know that they will only act as a starting point. In the Cloud world, customer expectations will be very different and you can assume that your requirements will change significantly. You may have to start thinking about how you will define more realistic specifications for a Cloud product that sells. |
| ☐ | 6.5.12 Is there a customer to help you? | It may be great to partner with one or more of your existing customers or prospects that can help you define your Cloud offering. Starting with a large customer offers the promise of a big win initially that can help provide the right marketing ammunition to launch the offering. However, they may suck up all your time and your offering may end up becoming a point solution. Start with your SMB customers. They will provide more opportunity to refine your offering. And, the risk is far lower. |
| ☐ | 6.5.13 Are your sales teams excited about the Cloud? | They may be skeptical because of a new product and new markets or because of a potential reduction in upfront commissions. On the other hand, they may be initially excited since they may see the Cloud product as a tool that can provide competitive advantage in the sales process. In reality, it may be a combination of the two. Having these discussions up front will be important to prepare the sales teams, since they will need to be key stakeholders in your Cloud initiative. |

| ☒ | Question | Why this matters |
|---|----------|------------------|
| ☐ | 6.5.14 When should we get our marketing team involved? | Yes, you will market your service after it's built. But you do need to figure out what the target market is, so your product can be tailored to their needs. It's also important to leverage the salesforce.com customer base, or a segment of it, for your product. Your marketing team will be a key stakeholder in your development initiative. They will the ones ultimately determining your targeted customer segment(s) and their needs. |
| ☐ | 6.5.15 Who will be leading your Cloud development effort? | If your Architect or Product Lead has been chosen to lead this effort, you need to think again. They will be very important to this effort, no doubt. To be successful, however, this has to be approached as a business transformation where you may redefine your customer segments, products as well as your marketing, sales and support. The leader of this initiative must be a senior stakeholder who is committed to driving revenue through your Cloud product. |
| ☐ | 6.5.16 How will all the stakeholders be engaged? | In addition to your product and technical team, it will be critical to turn Marketing and Sales into key stakeholders. How will you ensure that they put 'skin in the game' early in the development process, so they have an incentive to make this successful? |

2

| ☒ | Question | Why this matters |
|---|---|---|
| ☐ | 6.5.17 Will you hire consultants to help you? | Most ISVs tend to look at consultants through a technical prism - they look for a vendor to provide just the Force.com development expertise, turning your transition into a technical exercise. If you go that route, you may have a product but not too many customers. In reality, you will need a partner, not a vendor. The partner does need to provide the Force.com technical expertise required. But, more importantly, the partner must provide guidance on what will sell, how to reduce your ongoing costs as well as leadership through all aspects of the transformation. There are as many business challenges to cope with as there are technical issues. |
| ☐ | 6.5.18 How will you pick the consultant? | Since your consultant will be very critical to your success, you can't just pick one based on an RFP process if you want to avoid ending up with a scapegoat. The best approach is to pick someone who is willing to put skin in the game, in return for being rewarded for your commercial success. |
| ☐ | 6.5.19 Have you thought about a third party taking on customer facing roles? | *"You can either become a service provider yourself (not easy, and not cheap as it requires you to retool, reskill, and reorganize). Or, you can partner with a service provider to deliver your software as a service or to build services on top of your software and then deliver those,"* according to Daryl Plummer of Gartner. There are several trade-offs involved here but you may also want to think about letting a service provider assume the front-line role, managing development, marketing, sales and support for the first few years until you get your first 100 customers. |

## 6.6 How your organization will need to change

Moving to Cloud Computing is no small undertaking - it will impact the entire organization. It starts with the education and buy-in from the Board, investors and non-execs. Remember - "The confused mind says 'No.'

Then there is the organizational structure to consider. If Cloud Computing is being offered alongside a traditional offering do you need one schizophrenic organization or two parallel organizations, or even a separate division or company?

Much of this will be driven by the Go To Market (GTM) plans you have for your Cloud Computing offering, compared with those for your existing offering. The greater the difference, the more likely the disruption.

It may also be good to ask about the companies in your sector that have made the shift successfully? What can you learn from those who have failed to transition? Are there better examples in other sectors? Whilst new start-ups will have a far easier ride as they are starting with a clean sheet, they may still be great examples.

You will be providing a service. Your customers will be relying on you supporting their business 24 x 7 x 365. Your management team will now need a different set of information to manage the business and customers.

That information is new – SLA reporting, usage statistics, resource consumption. Some of this information is required internally to bill customers and reconcile billing from salesforce.com. Some of it may be need to be presented externally for customers. And all this is a cost to the business so it needs to be cheap, effective and scale. Do you have the processes and technology in place to do this, or do you need to build them?

| ☒ | Question | Why this matters |
|---|----------|------------------|
| ☐ | 6.6.1 Will this affect your legal structure? | You may wish to separate the Cloud offering into a separate business, JV or brand. Or it may become an extension of your existing offerings with no organizational change. Do you have plans to exit either the existing or the new Cloud business space? Will one legal structure over another simplify this in the future? |
| ☐ | 6.6.2 How will internal team relationships change? | Your sales and marketing people will probably have fewer touch points with customers. The development team will be working to a much more agile time frame for releases. Your customer success & support teams may be in closer contact with the customer. Support can provide feedback to development as well as be a major source of sales opportunities. All in all, there will be significant changes in your organization that you may need to plan for. |
| ☐ | 6.6.3 Have you thought about a customer success program? | Since it is in your interest to retain your customers so they continue to pay you, you will need to create a program to make sure your customers are happy with your service. In addition to providing periodic training, you may have to proactively reach out to your customers on a regular basis to pre-empt any issues, dissatisfaction or unmet needs. You may require a separate team that gets to know your customers more closely and focus on their success. |

| ☒ | Question | Why this matters |
|---|----------|------------------|
| ☐ | 6.6.4 Do you have mechanisms to capture customer feedback? | Your customers will be the best people to guide you on your product strategy going forward. In addition to the customer success initiatives, you may also want to understand which features of your product customers find most useful as well as any features that may be inadequate or missing. This can help you plan future versions of your product. To get this feedback on an ongoing basis, you will have to put together mechanisms and forums that work best for you. |
| ☐ | 6.6.5 What are your plans for recruitment, retention and departures? | This may be a time for change and it is highly likely that you will have to hire new people, ask some to leave and worry about retaining key people who cannot see the benefits of the new plan. This will happen, don't let it catch you unawares. |
| ☐ | 6.6.6 What will your partner model be? | Partnering grows in importance in the Cloud world. This is with respect to salesforce.com, your sales channels as well as ISVs with complimentary offerings. Will you sell the Cloud offering direct or via partners? If you have existing partners, are they capable of selling your Cloud offering? |
| ☐ | 6.6.7 Will Board meetings need to change frequency? | The business may be running to a different rhythm driven by monthly billing and regular product releases versus the focus on the annual product release and the annual chase for maintenance renewals. Does the board need to change their approach to frequency or content for meetings? |

| ☒ | Question | Why this matters |
|---|----------|------------------|
| ☐ | 6.6.8 Does your risk management culture need to change? | The increase in business rhythm is likely to require quick decision making, and a focus on risk management rather than risk avoidance. Is this something that is already in place, or will it need new skills? |
| ☐ | 6.6.9 Are new business metrics needed for the board? | Do you need to be measuring retention, user penetration per customer, speed of up sell from trials? Will your top line revenue stop being a useful measure if you are receiving referral revenue rather than full value with a cost of sale deduction? Does cost of invoicing vs. revenue become critical or the support cost per customer? |
| ☐ | 6.6.10 How will relations with investors change? | Your revenue profile may change significantly. This may be perceived as good or bad, with short and long term questions. Will you need to ask for short term funding as you move to an annuity revenue stream? Your existing investors may not be comfortable with this model, but other investors may suddenly be interested in you. |
| ☐ | 6.6.11 How does the marketing team's role change? | Where does marketing stop and sales start? Is marketing responsible for driving demand or only raising awareness? Most likely, your marketing team will start playing a much larger role in driving both awareness and demand. In fact, they will need to become key stakeholders in your Cloud initiative, starting from the concept stage. |

| ☒ | Question | Why this matters |
|---|----------|------------------|
| ☐ | 6.6.12  Will your accounting and other internal systems be able to support the Cloud initiative? | If you are changing from a low volume, high customer touch business, to a high volume, low touch one this may have significant implications for all your internal systems.  Micro billing, credit card payments, automated service provisioning tools, linked to accounts and support etc. |
| ☐ | 6.6.13  What changes will be required for accounting procedures and processes? | A license or maintenance fee with revenue recognition over twelve months could be replaced by monthly invoices and immediate recognition.  What about cross charges if you have different legal entities with their associated accounts?  Will you need to account for overseas sales, multiple currencies and differing tax regimes?  Will the budgeting cycle need to change from annual to quarterly, to mirror the more dynamic nature of the business? |
| ☐ | 6.6.14  What changes will be required for invoicing? | Changing from a single annual high value invoice to 12 low value ones, with a significantly increased customer population, can create huge invoicing challenges.  The cost of invoicing can quickly become a significant percentage of the invoice value. |
| ☐ | 6.6.15  Do you need to consider factoring? | If cash flow is an issue then it could help to consider some form of factoring to get the cash up front and let another party have the problems of cash collection, debt management etc. |
| ☐ | 6.6.16  Do your current auditors have the correct skills? | Your existing auditors may be excellent, but can they support you with a new business model as you grow internationally, with multiple tax regimes and complex R&D funding tax credits? |

| ☒ | Question | Why this matters |
|---|----------|------------------|
| ☐ | 6.6.17 Is there a tax benefit associated with your Cloud initiative? | Governments around the world are encouraging businesses to engage in research through the use of tax incentives and grant funding. It may be that the development of your Cloud offering could benefit from one of these programs. |
| ☐ | 6.6.18 Do you have the correct skills to communicate your new market positioning? | Your current marketing team (whether internal or external) will have the skills to work in your current geography /industry/product. Do they have the skills if you are reaching out to new geographies, or entering new industries? |
| ☐ | 6.6.19 How will yours partners make money? | Does a partner buy the Cloud offering for a discount from list and contract directly? Or do you contract with the customer and the partner gets a referral? Can the partner build value add on your offering and sell this? |
| ☐ | 6.6.20 Will your Cloud offering cause channel conflict? | If you sell direct will this be in conflict with your existing channel? Also, you sell direct will this be in conflict with the salesforce.com direct sales teams? If you sell through new partners, but not all of the existing ones, why not? Is the pricing for the Cloud offering disruptive to your existing products? |

| ☒ | Question | Why this matters |
|---|----------|------------------|
| ☐ | 6.6.21 Do your sales incentive plans reflect the new revenue models? | The customer has signed a 3 year contract, based on monthly payments and an option to leave at any time with 3 month's notice. Do you reward your sales person upfront and hope the customer stays? Do you reward as income arrives, so the sales person builds an ongoing book of commission rewards? Whilst the annuity revenue models are driving this discussion there is also a wider social desire to see people rewarded for long term success rather than short term wins. |
| ☐ | 6.6.22 Is your sales team able to adapt? | For some sales people these changes may be too much; longer term incentive schemes, a need to engage with customers through different mediums and via different contact points (business rather than IT) and dealing with customers who have been able to self educate via the web. For others the change may be easy and a breath of fresh air. However, as with any change, do not underestimate the potential for disruption. It may be that your current top salesperson will have a lot to lose and could become one of the major roadblocks to change – or worse, leaves to go to the competition. |
| ☐ | 6.6.23 Does your sales team have the tools needed to demo your offering? | Do your sales team need laptops with 3G mobile broadband so they can demo the offering? What about smart phones to show the mobile capability? Can they setup demo accounts for the customer? How do you handle low touch engagements? Can you offer web based conferences? Can the potential customer run their own demo session from your web site? |

| ☒ | Question | Why this matters |
|---|----------|------------------|
| ☐ | 6.6.24  Does your implementation team have the correct skills balance? | It is likely that a key skill has been the installation and setup of servers and software at customer sites. This will reduce significantly. Do you have the skills to now offer more training, consulting, business process change and systems integration? The money is still there, however you may have to offer different services to get it. Can you do that across various new geographies that you may have to cover? Do you need partnerships with other services vendors? |
| ☐ | 6.6.25  Do you need overseas implementation partners? | Even with a hosted only offering it is likely that there will be services required by the customer on site (training, integration etc). If you are expanding into overseas markets do you grow your own services business to deliver this or do you look to partner with other organizations (local or global) that can offer this service and provide a margin to you? |
| ☐ | 6.6.26  How will you manage the changing role of support? | The customer success & support teams will potentially be your main human contact with the customer. They could be an excellent source of up sell sales leads and ideas for product development. Is the support team lead involved in weekly sales planning meetings? Are they invited to development and product roadmap reviews? Is the support team motivated and rewarded for identifying these opportunities? Remember they are not sales people and will probably need different incentives. Support is likely to change from being a cost centre that is targeted with keeping the customer happy, to a strategic asset within the business. |

| ☒ | Question | Why this matters |
|---|---|---|
| ☐ | 6.6.27 What investment is required to provide customer support the tools they need? | If your support team is going to provide sales leads and development ideas to the business, how is this managed so it doesn't become a paper overhead? Do they have access to the sales tracking system? Should you implement a companywide CRM - Salesforce perhaps? |
| ☐ | 6.6.28 How will you manage the SLAs on the customer and salesforce.com side? | Even though you sold your app to customers as a product company, they will look at you as a service provider. That means managing SLAs. This is something you may not have dealt with before. Some of the SLAs may be part of your contract and some of them may be inherent in the Cloud model. For instance, since your customers will be paying you on a monthly / quarterly / annually basis they may be having certain expectations without you being aware. Similarly, there will be several aspects of service delivery to your customers that will be the responsibility of salesforce.com. You will need to understand all of these SLAs and put together a plan to manage them. |
| ☐ | 6.6.29 Do you have a team to manage provisioning of trials & production orgs? | Your sales teams may come to you if a prospect is interested in getting a free trial of your service. Similarly customers signing contracts with you will need production orgs of Force.com (or Salesforce CRM), with your app installed. Salesforce.com provides tools for your teams to able to manage all of this. You will need to understand everything that needs to be done to manage this effectively on an ongoing basis. |

| ☒ | Question | Why this matters |
|---|----------|------------------|
| ☐ | 6.6.30 Will you manage OEM customers as well as co-sell customers? | The responsibility for supporting a customer may be different depending on whether they are your direct customer (as a reseller) or whether they bought the Force.com seats from salesforce.com (co-sell model). If you will be supporting both models, you will need to understand how the support responsibilities will be different depending on the model, and plan accordingly. |
| ☐ | 6.6.31 How will you manage seat counts and expiration dates? | You will need to monitor your customers and how they use your app. You will need to keep a close tab on their contracts and seat counts. Salesforce.com provides a License Management App (LMA) for you to monitor all of this. Using LMA, you will have to create an internal process to deal with it proactively. |
| ☐ | 6.6.32 Will you be creating release notes for your releases? | For every release, you will have to create elaborate release notes, so that your customers can upgrade as well as utilize the new functionality without putting too much burden on your training and support teams. If you do this right, it can save you significant time and money. |

| ☒ | Question | Why this matters |
|---|----------|------------------|
| ☐ | 6.6.33 How will you establish a Tier 3 support process with salesforce.com? | There will be some support requests that may be related to features provided by salesforce.com. If you are a reseller, you will have to reach out to salesforce.com support for such requests on behalf of your customers. The resolution to such requests will be outside of your control. Bouncing around support requests can be very frustrating to customers. You will have to create a seamless process to get these requests resolved in a reasonable timeframe as well we manage communications with your customers. |

# Chapter 7

# Questions for jeans

*It should be possible to explain the laws of physics to a barmaid.*

**Albert Einstein (Scientist, 1879 - 1955)**

MOVING into the Cloud may appear very simple, if you believe all the hype. There are dozens of "Cloud converters" being peddled today that can supposedly get you there in days or weeks. They promise to enable you to migrate your idea or spreadsheet or an existing on-premise product into the Cloud with the click of a few buttons.

Is it really that straightforward? No, we're not there yet. If we're lucky, maybe in the next 5 – 10 years, this may become a simple "transportation" problem. Simple enough for American Airlines, UPS or even Two Men and A Truck to move you into the Cloud. Until then, you, the architect, will need to do some very heavy lifting.

Because it's a different way of running your business, Cloud Computing will require a fresh mindset as you start thinking about your product architecture, development methodology, customer deployment, maintenance, upgrades and support. And more importantly, you will also have to think about how to meet customer expectations when they will be "renting" from you as opposed to "buying".

You will do a big favor to your organization by understanding all the implications first. So if you haven't at least skim-read the previous chapter – go back and do it now.

## 7.1 The big picture

Before you get into architecture and design, there are some fundamental considerations around your current product, target customers, Force.com and the development environment. These may then help you think through the more detailed questions you need to be asking.

So, let's jump in and do a quick "sanity check" first.

| ☒ | Question | Why this matters |
|---|----------|------------------|
| ☐ | 7.1.1 Why would you build on Force.com if it's cheaper to build on Java or .Net? | People ask us this question all the time. In certain situations they realize that the cost of building an app on, say, the .Net platform is lower, particularly if it has a significant web component. But it will cost much more to turn that into a multi-tenant Cloud app that can be commercially sold, managed and supported. A comparison between Force.com and Azure may be a more apt one if you are looking to build a Cloud app cost effectively. In future, VMForce may offer the ability to build a Cloud app in Java. |
| ☐ | 7.1.2 What are the alternatives to Force.com? | If you want to use a PaaS, there are other platforms that you can look into – Microsoft's Azure is the most talked about alternative. However, Azure hasn't clearly spelled out how multi-tenancy, which will be an absolute must, will be supported. There are also Cloud accelerators that can help you create your own private Cloud. |
| ☐ | 7.1.3 How can you determine if Force.com is the right platform for you? | You will probably not win an award for asking this question since everyone else does too. You will need to create a set of criteria based on your requirements. However, in addition to technical features, there are other important factors that will determine the suitability too. For instance, is the salesforce.com customer base an easy target for you? Will getting married to salesforce.com be the right cultural fit? |

| ☒ | Question | Why this matters |
|---|----------|------------------|
| ☐ | 7.1.4 Is this a new development with no legacy? | This is a new idea, no legacy, no constraints, no existing customers pushing you one way or the other. Essentially you are a start up with the freedoms that this brings. In some ways, it may be easier for you to build a Cloud-based model for your company from scratch. However you also have nothing to benchmark yourself against, everything is new and there will be many unexpected hurdles to jump over. Freedom can come at a heavy price. |
| ☐ | 7.1.5 You have an existing on premise app. Is there an easy way to convert it to Force.com? | No. You must avoid this trap for so many reasons. It will be a complete re-write. Also, you must challenge yourself and find a sound rationale for 'converting' an existing app into a Force.com service since it won't be well received by your customers. You will have to redefine your value proposition and your features/functions, before you build a Cloud product. |
| ☐ | 7.1.6 Are there any legacy components that need to be used? | Use of a managed platform such as Force.com comes at the cost of some level of control and flexibility. As you don't have access to the operating system you cannot run third party applications and services on Force.com (this may change with VMforce). You will be forced to re-write any legacy functionality if you'd like it to run natively in salesforce.com's Cloud. Otherwise you may need to think about a composite app where the legacy components will run on another platform and be integrated to the Force.com app. |

| ☒ | Question | Why this matters |
|---|----------|------------------|
| ☐ | 7.1.7 Are you replacing an existing offering? | If you are replacing an existing legacy offering, you can be certain that customers of your Force.com service will expect something different. First, because they may be from a different market segment. Secondly, they will demand constant improvement. Thirdly, their expectations may also be related to features provided by salesforce.com, as opposed to your product. You can safely assume you will need to revisit your offering in the Cloud. |
| ☐ | 7.1.8 Do you want to productize your existing Salesforce implementation into a commercial product? | You may have implemented Salesforce CRM or Force.com successfully for your organization and may now be thinking of converting your implementation into a commercial product and selling it to other companies like yours and making some money on it. The CIO in Case 7 of Chapter 1 also had the same idea. It's possible, but it will be incredibly difficult. The design of a commercial app is entirely different from the design of an implementation for a single customer; just the way cooking in a restaurant environment is different from cooking at home. |

| ☒ | Question | Why this matters |
|---|----------|------------------|
| ☐ | 7.1.9 Will your app be based on a single org or a distributed org model? | If your product idea is a portal that your customers will be accessing through the web, your app will reside on a single org of Salesforce or Force.com. In that case, you will technically be a customer of salesforce.com and buy the appropriate Force.com and portal seats to implement your app. If, however, each of your customers will install and run your app in their own Force.com production environment, you will be building a distributed org model as a salesforce.com partner or reseller. In this model, your customers will buy your packaged app from you, and take advantage of the administration and customization capabilities native to the Force.com platform. |

| ☒ | Question | Why this matters |
|---|----------|------------------|
| ☐ | 7.1.10  Will your app be native or composite? | You can build your app natively, which means that the app functionality, logic, user interface and data will reside on Force.com or one of salesforce.com's strategic partners. These partners include Google, Amazon and Facebook as of today. A native app offers the advantages of higher scalability, lower infrastructure and maintenance costs, better marketing opportunities and increased security that may be important to your customers. In addition, a native app can also be fully multi-tenant. Non-native apps, known as composite or client apps, typically rely on the Force.com Web services API to integrate with Salesforce CRM or the Force.com platform. If you are planning to build a composite app, you will need to think through how you will provide upgrades, provide infrastructure (security, data backups etc.), maintenance and also, most importantly, multi-tenancy. |
| ☐ | 7.1.11  If you build an app natively, can it also run independently on the Google, Amazon or Facebook platforms? | No. You can have components of your app run on any of these platforms. However, each component will only run on the platform that you develop it for. Trying to build an app that can run on all of these platforms will be difficult and expensive. You may have to think carefully through the reasons for which you want to develop a certain component for, say, Facebook and determine the extra costs involved. |

| ☒ | Question | Why this matters |
|---|----------|------------------|
| ☐ | 7.1.12 Is it more expensive to build a native app, as opposed to a composite app? | The answer isn't simple. If you're starting from scratch and the available Force.com features meet your needs, it may be more cost effective to build your app natively. If, however, you already have pieces of your app built on another platform, it may sometimes be less expensive to create a composite app that integrates through the Force.com API. |
| ☐ | 7.1.13 Will your app be an extension to Salesforce CRM or a standalone app? | This is an important decision you will need to make. If your app uses standard objects, such as Opportunities and Cases, that are available with Salesforce CRM but not with Force.com, you will be extending Salesforce CRM. In that scenario, you will be dependent on salesforce.com Account Managers to sell Salesforce seats (minimum of one) to your customer before you can sell you app. Your app will only run on Salesforce editions that provide the standard objects that your app uses. If, however, the only standard objects that your app uses are the ones provided by Force.com, your app can be an independent platform app which can be bundled with Force.com seats and sold directly by you as a salesforce.com VAR or OEM partner. |

| ☒ | Question | Why this matters |
|---|----------|------------------|
| ☐ | 7.1.14 Are you incorporating 3$^{rd}$ party services (mashups)? | Using 3$^{rd}$ party services can be a quick way to provide significant capability to your service. An example would be using Live Earth or Google Maps as a way to present geospatial reports within your offering. However the APIs for these are likely to change over time or the service may cease to be available. How do you manage testing and replacement. What happens if the service has not ceased but is less reliable than desired? Many of these services are popular because they are free; however this is also likely to limit the amount of documentation and support available. |
| ☐ | 7.1.15 Are you confident that the engineering level is appropriate to the customer need? | Just because we can design and build a Rolls Royce solution does not make it the right approach. Your product idea (or your existing on-premise product) may be very complex and it may be tempting to build an all-encompassing app that can become a killer product. However, customer expectations are very different in the Cloud world. You may want to think about creating a broad foundation and framework, with reduced functionality in the first phase, so you can get feedback from customers. |
| ☐ | 7.1.16 Will your IP be protected? | Managed packages help you protect your IP by obfuscating app logic and UI. You can hide the code in certain components and your design must take that into account. You must figure out the components that facilitate code obfuscation and see if that meets your IP protection requirements. |

| ☒ | Question | Why this matters |
|---|----------|------------------|
| ☐ | 7.1.17 Are you also targeting existing salesforce.com customers? | If your prospect already uses Salesforce CRM or Force.com, your product will also need to work as a plug-in without disrupting any configurations/customizations they may already have. If you need to handle such situations, it will change your design so as to avoid disruptions to the customer's existing Salesforce or Force.com org. It may also have an impact on your financial model since you may be sharing revenue and support responsibilities. |
| ☐ | 7.1.18 Does your pricing model change your solution architecture? | It's very important to take into account what your customers will pay for your app, before you design your app. For instance, if your customers will be able to pay only $25 per user every month, you will need to come up with a design that requires minimum implementation, maintenance and support time, so you can keep your costs low. |
| ☐ | 7.1.19 Are there any geographical restrictions to be aware of? | There are no geographical restrictions, if you are deploying a native app built on Force.com. If you are building a composite app, the restrictions, if any, would depend on the content that you put on servers outside of salesforce.com and their location. |

| ☒ | Question | Why this matters |
|---|----------|------------------|
| ☐ | 7.1.20  Do you need to ensure that users store data in a data center in their region? | Salesforce.com has data centers in multiple regions. However, there will not be a data center in every country. Consider whether there are legal restrictions on where data can be stored. Consider also customer preferences and how you manage their data. Consider whether your application needs to be able to store data in a particular region for certain customers. |

## 7.2 Designing your product

Beyond the big picture, you need to think through the factors that will influence the architecture of your product so you can start compiling that information.

Some of these are the fundamental ones at the heart of any product design. How can you build it as quickly as possible so that it can be maintained and extended easily? Can you provide a compelling user experience without compromising performance when accessed via every browser currently available and planned?

Next, you will be asking some critical questions that can make or break your entire Cloud business. How can you create a salesforce.com-like multi-tenant model for your customers so you can have a common code base to serve your customers? Will your architecture permit you to fix a bug and roll out to all your customers in one stroke? Will you be able to roll out a new release seamlessly?

Oh, and by the way, all this must be in Release 1.0.

This section, therefore, has all the important questions you need to consider, to balance these inevitable compromises.

| ☒ | Question | Why this matters |
|---|----------|------------------|
| ☐ | 7.2.1 What factors will impact the design? | Typically in any product design, there are several fundamental aspects that will determine the design of your app, such as functionality, custom code and screens, ability to maintain, enhance and support. The Force.com world will be no different. You will have to list your priorities upfront. One of the most critical pieces of design is the data model and it is important to get it right. |
| ☐ | 7.2.2 What factors will impact the data model? | The primary ones impacting the data model are functional requirements, reporting requirements, security/permissions requirements and calculations/rules. Since the data model is extremely critical, the more requirements you can list upfront, the better. |
| ☐ | 7.2.3 Will the Force.com security and permissions model be sufficient? | You will need to provide the ability to set security permissions for users based on various rules (e.g. based on their role in the organization they may only be able to view certain fields but not edit them). Force.com provides a built-in set of security permissions that can be used. However, there may be situations where this security model may not suffice. Let's say you have four objects connected to each other. A user with access to one of the objects may need to automatically have access to the other three objects. In a situation like this, you will need to extend the Force.com security model. This may become a significant part of your design, to be figured out upfront. |

| ☒ | Question | Why this matters |
|---|----------|------------------|
| ☐ | 7.2.4 Will your product be multi-tenant, since you're building on Force.com? | Just because you are developing a product on Force.com, it doesn't mean it will become multi-tenant automatically. Force.com does provide multi-tenancy (a mechanism for you to build a multi-tenant product) at the infrastructure level. This is accomplished through managed packages, discussed in the next question. However, you will still need to build multi-tenancy at the application level - this will be an important part of your design. |
| ☐ | 7.2.5 Will your customers be able to get upgrades to your product? | Yes. As a matter of fact, that's a huge advantage of building a commercial product on Force.com. Managed packages allow your customers to upgrade to a new version of your product without losing their data or customizations. In addition, they enable you to protect your IP, as well as monitor and manage your customers using the License Management App (LMA). Using managed packages will be a very important architectural consideration for you since they will require you to *lock down* components of your app, requiring a flexibility trade-off. |

| ☒ | Question | Why this matters |
|---|----------|------------------|
| ☐ | 7.2.6 Is there additional cost and effort required to package your cloud product? | Yes. Packaging your app isn't as simple as creating a PDF file from a Word document. It can add significantly to the cost (and timeline) of development. There isn't a cookie-cutter approach to this since a lot depends on the analysis and thought process you will need to go through. This analysis is critical since the features that are part of a managed package cannot be modified by your customers. The packaging effort also depends on the complexity of the pieces that you decide to package. However, you can assume that packaging will increase the initial development costs by 25% to 100%, depending on a variety of factors. |
| ☐ | 7.2.7 Can you build your app and roll it out without packaging it? | You can, indeed. However, it won't be a multi-tenant app, which means that each customer will have their own version of your app, creating a maintenance, support and upgrade nightmare for you. As your customer base grows, the cost of managing the versions will be too high and you will likely go out of business. |
| ☐ | 7.2.8 Can you build your app, roll it out to two customers and deal with packaging after? | Once again, you can. However, you will have to migrate your first two customers to the packaged version of your product later, if you want them to benefit from your upgrades for subsequent versions. There may be significant costs involved in this migration which your customers may not be willing to bear. Even though you will spend extra money and effort with this approach, sometimes the experience gained with live customers may be helpful in figuring out what to package and lock down. |

| ☒ | Question | Why this matters |
|---|----------|------------------|
| ☐ | 7.2.9 Can you use any of the features that Force.com provides, in your product? | You can use any of the features in your product. However, not all features can be part of a managed package. With every release of the Force.com platform, more and more features become *packageable*. It's important to understand early on what features can be packaged in the current release, if you want to take advantage of managed packages - otherwise you will have to rewrite your app. |
| ☐ | 7.2.10 Can sections of the service be easily replaced (loosely coupled, highly cohesive)? | If you envision building an entire suite of products, you may want to consider creating common modules that can be used across multiple products. This will enable you to save on maintenance, support and upgrades. You will also need to create a packaging architecture for these modules, to facilitate upgrades. |
| ☐ | 7.2.11 Is the product related to other products you may be launching on Force.com? | If the product is part of a suite of products being offered then the interaction and integration between all the products need to be considered as part of the design. For instance, if a customer wants to buy two of your products that are both built on Force.com, you will need a more integrated product design upfront. |

| ☒ | Question | Why this matters |
|---|----------|------------------|
| ☐ | 7.2.12 How is connectivity built in both internally and externally? | If you service is going to talk to other components of your offering or connect with 3<sup>rd</sup> parties then you need to consider how the communications will be handled. Using the Force.com API, your customers may be able to build these integrations themselves but that can be time consuming and expensive for every customer. You may want to plan for this integration in the product design, if you know about these systems in advance. |
| ☐ | 7.2.13 How is redundancy handled? | Things go wrong. Hardware fails. There are many ways to provide redundancy. If you build your product natively, then the Force.com platform handles the data backups and redundancy for you. However, if you build a composite product, you will need your own plan and infrastructure for data backups and redundancy for the components of your app that do not reside in salesforce.com's Cloud. |
| ☐ | 7.2.14 Do you have a need for data aggregation or exchange across your customer base? | If some data from all your customers needs to be aggregated into a centralized place then it may require creation of another Force.com org that acts as the data repository. The data repository can receive data from all customer orgs, process the data, and also provide summary/analysis back to each customer org, if required. Depending on whether the need is for data aggregation or exchange, you will need to work on a design such that everything is hosted in salesforce.com's cloud, for it to be scalable. |

| ☒ | Question | Why this matters |
|---|----------|------------------|
| ☐ | 7.2.15 Will your customers have external users (or their customers) accessing the product? | If external users (i.e. your customer's customers), that will not be provided Force.com logins, will be accessing the product through the internet, there are two licensing options available today. These two options, Force.com Sites and Customer Portal, provide various editions that you can pick from, depending on your needs. Your entire product will continue to be hosted on salesforce.com's Cloud if you go with either of these options. Irrespective of whether Sites or Customer Portal is used, your customers will want to have control over the look & feel of their external pages, provide their own branding etc. If you need to provide such flexibility to your customers within a native app, there will be several critical design implications. |
| ☐ | 7.2.16 Can components Force.com Sites or Customer Portal be part of a Managed Package? | Yes. You will be able to build all web pages using Visualforce, for a compelling user interface. All the pages can be part of a Managed Package. |

| ☒ | Question | Why this matters |
|---|----------|------------------|
| ☐ | 7.2.17  Which salesforce.com editions will your product support? | There are various salesforce.com editions such as Group, Unlimited, Enterprise, Professional as well as Force.com Editions such as Free, Enterprise, Unlimited that salesforce.com customers may be using. This decision must be made based on the market segment that you want to target. Once you decide which editions your product will support you will need to determine the features provided by each of those editions (you can get this information from *online help*). Since you'll be developing in a Developer Edition environment, which has access to many features not necessarily available in the customer edition, you will be designing according to the editions you'd want your product to run on. |
| ☐ | 7.2.18  Are your customers looking for a rich user experience, different from the standard salesforce.com interface? | The Force.com native interface works in a specific way. Your customers may or may not like the native Force.com user interface. Using Visualforce and other third-party (such as Adobe) tools, you can create any kind of user experience desired. The trade-off, however, will be increased development/ maintenance costs. You will also be reducing your customer's ability to customize, if you go with custom screens. In addition, you will need to check if the third-party tools that you want to use, are packageable. |
| ☐ | 7.2.19  Can you hire professional creative designers to create rich user interfaces? | Yes, you can. If your design is right, you can use creative design firms to develop your web page designs. These can be incorporated within Visualforce pages. |

| ☒ | Question | Why this matters |
|---|----------|------------------|
| ☐ | 7.2.20 How comfortable would existing users be in moving to a different interface? | If you are moving existing customers from another platform to Force.com you need to figure out if they will be open to a different look and feel. Recreating the exact look and feel of the existing platform may not be prudent – it may lead to design deficiencies and maintenance overhead. |
| ☐ | 7.2.21 Have you defined the reporting needs? | A common mistake is to build the product and think of reporting later. However, on the Force.com platform, reporting requirements impact design. They can have an impact on how tables are linked and de-normalized, as well as how code is written. This is because the Force.com reporting engine may have limitations on the number of objects that can be linked up, based on the relationships between objects. Depending on the reports required, your design will need to make all the required fields available for reporting. |
| ☐ | 7.2.22 Are your reporting needs more complex than what Force.com can currently handle? | Force.com provides you a very robust reporting engine that users with no technical experience can easily use. If your needs go beyond that, you may also be able to bundle other third party reporting products that are integrated with Force.com. There are some Cloud-based options available and more in the works. You will need to determine if the chosen option is packageable. |

| ☒ | Question | Why this matters |
|---|----------|------------------|
| ☐ | 7.2.23 Do you need to build complex calculations? | In a Force.com environment, the system resources are shared so you need to think through governor limits, number of queries, API calls etc. as you design the product. Often, complex calculations require multiple queries to get the input data, perform the calculation and then make multiple updates. Depending on the type of calculations, the frequency of calculations and the number of updates, the system resources need to be managed and factored in the design. |
| ☐ | 7.2.24 Are there high performance / low latency requirements within your application | If your application is going to be a high-performance transactional messaging system you need to carefully consider whether Force.com is appropriate. By using Force.com you are trading simplicity for control. You may not be able to throttle, control or shape network traffic in the same way as you can, when you create and own the infrastructure. Consider if this could adversely affect performance for your users or application. |
| ☐ | 7.2.25 Does the service need to be multi-lingual? | The Cloud means, in theory, anyone anywhere in the world can access the application. Although many people have English as their native or second language not everyone will be comfortable with English. Depending on your user base, you may want to provide multi-lingual capability. The good news is that Force.com has built-in tools that can be used to switch to different languages based on the user's preferences. You will, however, need to provide the corresponding word translation for every custom field. |

| ☒ | Question | Why this matters |
|---|----------|------------------|
| ☐ | 7.2.26 What is the impact of session state with Force.com? | Salesforce.com supports session management features with timeouts. These features are available with Salesforce, Force.com as well as Customer or Partner portal. However, you won't be getting full-fledged transaction processing capabilities typically supported by a TP Monitor. |
| ☐ | 7.2.27 Will you allow 3$^{rd}$ party developers to extend your product? | Will you allow access to an environment and documentation that will enable 3$^{rd}$ parties to extend the application? Are 3$^{rd}$ parties able to customize or configure the service for customers? You may even be offering a small part of your service so it can be part of somebody else's mashup. If you offer these capabilities, how will you manage maintenance and upgrades? |
| ☐ | 7.2.28 Do you want customers to be able to download other third party products from AppExchange? | If so, you will have to sign the appropriate contract with salesforce.com. Otherwise, any enhancements to your product needed by a customer will have to be handled as customizations. Of course, you can also offer your product as a plug-in, where you will co-sell with salesforce.com Account Executives. In that situation, you will also need to work on an open design so your app can work on all Salesforce and Force.com editions as well as plug in with most 3$^{rd}$ party applications. |
| ☐ | 7.2.29 Will your customers need mobile access? | The great news is that you will be able to offer pre-built mobile versions of your app on devices such as Blackberry and iPhone, without doing too much extra work. There is cost associated with mobile access. You will need to understand the needs of mobile users and incorporate them for the mobile version. |

| ☒ | Question | Why this matters |
|---|----------|------------------|
| ☐ | 7.2.30 Do you need to offer offline as well as online capability? | What is the balance between the functionality which is on-line and available offline when connectivity is lost? Force.com provides an offline edition. However, all the features of your app may not be available in the offline version. If it is important for you to provide offline capability, then you need to first analyze which product features will not be supported in the offline edition. The next step may be to determine if that functionality can be provided with an alternative design that will work with the offline edition. |
| ☐ | 7.2.31 What customization will the customer be able to do? | With a Managed Package, the features of your product will be locked - the customers will not be able to make any changes that impact the functionality of your product. However, the customers will be able to extend your app by adding new functionality on top of the core product functionality. That's the reason why creating your managed package will be a very critical exercise. If you want to prevent the customers from making any enhancements, you will need to sell an embedded version of the platform and not provide any administrative capabilities to the customers. |

| ☒ | Question | Why this matters |
|---|----------|------------------|
| ☐ | 7.2.32  Will you provide tools for data migration? | It is important to make the customer's transition to your product as smooth as possible. Your customers will want you to figure out how their existing data will be migrated. There are a couple of options to consider - a) do you want to provide additional data migration services or b) do you want to build an automated tool to facilitate data migration. If you choose to go with option b, the data migration tool will be part of your design. |

## 7.3 Developing your product

The process of writing an application is a complex one. The languages/tools you use and the development processes you follow are big decisions. Once your application is written, how you manage new versions, manage testing and manage go-live is all vitally important.

Since Cloud is a 'service delivery' model, the application lifecycle involves more than just developing a version of the app. You will be responsible for creating a service that will continuously be maintained by your team. It will, therefore, be critical to revisit your Application Lifecycle Management process and supporting technology platform.

Before deciding if Force.com is appropriate you need to ask the following questions.

| ☒ | Question | Why this matters |
|---|----------|------------------|
| ☐ | 7.3.1 Do you have skills in the development environment and architecture? | Most organizations today have some experience working with salesforce.com. They may have an internal administrator, or even people who have coded using Apex. However, building a commercial product will be more than just programming in the Force.com environment. It will require a very different skill-set. You must understand what kind of expertise you will need before assuming it's just another platform or language. |
| ☐ | 7.3.2 To what level have your requirements been defined? | If you have a product idea or an existing on-premise product to migrate, you probably have a decent handle on what the requirements of your Force.com product are. However, you can safely assume that they will change significantly. This is because you will now have to rethink what your customers will find valuable from a service being rolled out on salesforce.com's platform, considering that there may be other complimentary features available or possible in future. You will also need to define requirements that are granular enough for Force.com experts to be able to size the first version of the product for you. In addition, your requirements need to be as comprehensive as possible, since rolling out upgrades to your customers, for a Force.com service, can become very expensive if the underlying product architecture changes. |

| ☒ | Question | Why this matters |
|---|----------|------------------|
| ☐ | 7.3.3 Do you have one of your existing or target customers to help you define customer needs? | Don't assume that you know your customers - the expectation from a Force-com based Cloud service will be very different from your on-premise product. One, your market segment may change. Two, your customers will demand constant improvement. Three, their expectations may also be related to features provided by salesforce.com. It's very important to know what your customers would want from your new service, before you build it and, therefore, requirements from your first few customers will be particularly critical. Do you have any existing (or prospective) customers that can help you? Is your relationship good enough for you to get what you need, without promising them too much? |
| ☐ | 7.3.4 How will new user requirements be captured and prioritized? | You will need to carefully manage the expectations of your first customers so they don't spiral out of control. Subsequently, you may have to use other mechanisms to capture requirements from customers, such as online feedback/voting and feedback from your support team. You will undoubtedly get significant feedback from your customers. It will be very critical to separate common requirements (that will be part of the core product) from requirements that may be unique to a certain customer (that must be handled through customizations). |

| ☒ | Question | Why this matters |
|---|----------|------------------|
| ☐ | 7.3.5 How will you manage the change cycle? | How do you manage the change cycle – from product roadmap strategy, user requirements, development, test and release? Can you provide traceability from user suggestion to the release in which it is implemented? This will ensure internal quality, but also offer confidence to your customers, regarding your approach. |
| ☐ | 7.3.6 Are you aware of customer expectations related to upgrades and new releases for a Force.com service? | Most on-premise offerings have a 6 to 12 month release cycle (or longer) with patches shipped in-between. There is cost and effort involved in installing upgrades and the cost is typically borne by customers. In the Cloud model, your customers will expect free upgrades that are seamlessly installed, just the way salesforce.com rolls out upgrades to the Force.com service. They will also expect you to help them with any issues as well as train the users on the features of the new release. All this can add up to significant cost overheads for you. In addition, if there are significant design changes in your new release, automatic updates may not even be possible leading to very high costs. You need to think through your release strategy and how to manage expectations of your customers as well as your sales teams. |

| ☒ | Question | Why this matters |
|---|----------|------------------|
| ☐ | 7.3.7 Will the salesforce.com upgrades affect your release schedules? | You can monitor the salesforce.com maintenance schedule by visiting trust.salesforce.com/trust/status and clicking the *View Upcoming Maintenance* Schedule link. There may also be different times for upgrading sandbox and production environments. You will need to make sure your development process doesn't get interrupted to maintenance downtime. You can also find out about new features in a release by clicking on the *What's New* link in the Help and Training window. More importantly, you can check with your salesforce.com Alliance Manager to see if you can create a plan for testing your product in advance, for the new release. |
| ☐ | 7.3.8 What development environments will be available to you? | The Force.com IDE is the most widely used development environment for those developing on salesforce.com's platform. It is built on the open-source Eclipse Platform and is great for developing apps using Apex, Visualforce, and other metadata components. It provides tools such as source code editors, test execution tools, deployment aids and integrated help. It supports most popular source code control systems, including Subversion. |

| ☒ | Question | Why this matters |
|---|----------|------------------|
| ☐ | 7.3.9 What languages are your developers skilled in using? | If your goal is to build an app natively on Force.com, you will need to use salesforce.com's proprietary Apex programming language for development (after VMforce is launched, you may be able to develop on Java – however, it remains to be seen how VMforce will support multi-tenancy and other PaaS must-haves). Apex is similar to any object oriented language, although there may still be a learning curve. You can also use HTML, Javascript or Adobe tools on the client side, in your native app. If you wish to use other languages, you will be able to but your app will be composite. A composite app on Force.com can support PHP, Ruby On Rails, Java, or .Net based languages such as C#, ASP.NET and Visual Basic. If you choose to build your app using one of these languages, you can avoid learning the entire Apex language and just learn the appropriate API calls. However, you will also need to check if your app will still be packageable. |
| ☐ | 7.3.10 Will you be able to use an ALM tool that you currently use? | There are a few ALM tools that currently plug into the Force.com development environment. You may be able to find them on AppExchange. You can also check with your vendor to see which steps of the Force.com Development Lifecycle your ALM tool supports, if any. |

| ☒ | Question | Why this matters |
|---|---|---|
| ☐ | 7.3.11 Will you need Developer Editions? | You will most probably be using Developer Edition orgs as your Development Environment. Developer Edition provides free access to many of the exclusive features available with Enterprise and Unlimited Editions. You get full access to the Force.com platform and API, so that you can extend the core features, integrate with other applications, and develop new tools and applications. However, salesforce.com does not provide support for Developer Edition Organizations. There are also certain limitations that a standard Developer Edition has such as number of licenses, API calls per day, storage etc. As a salesforce.com partner, you may be able to get some of these restrictions lifted, depending on your needs. Discuss with your Force.com Alliance Manager. |
| ☐ | 7.3.12 How many Developer Edition orgs will you need? | There is no silver bullet here. Several developers may still be able to code using one org. However, for a large project, you may want to have a Developer Edition org for each developer (they are free). You will be able to replicate metadata as well as any test data for each development org. You will also be able to create a separate integration org which can be used for bringing everyone's code and metadata together periodically, for integration testing. |

| ☒ | Question | Why this matters |
|---|----------|------------------|
| ☐ | 7.3.13 How many sandbox environments will you need? | You will use sandboxes in certain situations where you have a single production org serving all of your customers. You may also need sandboxes for certain customers that may want to test your product before you roll out a new upgrade. There are several types of sandboxes available - full sandboxes will be ideal for your customers to test your product. Creating or refreshing a sandbox copy can take several days so you will need to plan these in advance. There may also be costs involved. |
| ☐ | 7.3.14 How will you perform integration testing? | If you have multiple developers writing code, you will need to integrate all the code on a frequent basis, and test it. You will be able to use an open-source continuous integration tool called CruiseControl that will pull out code from the source control system and put it in an integration org. You will be able to define the frequency and CruiseControl will take care of assembling the code automatically. |
| ☐ | 7.3.15 How will you perform load testing? | If you develop a native app using only the standard Force.com feature set, there won't be any need for load testing - the Force.com cloud infrastructure will handle scalability. If you develop using third party tools such as ActiveWidgets or jQuery, or any other open source tools, lead testing will be needed. Load testing will also become critical, if you are developing a composite app. |

| ☒ | Question | Why this matters |
|---|---|---|
| ☐ | 7.3.16 How will you create customized versions of your app for specific customers? | With traditional on-premise application development it's very easy to create versions of your application with tweaks or additional functionality for individual customers. With a multi-tenant design offered by Force.com this is something you want to completely avoid since it will significantly increase your maintenance costs. You will need to think through your product strategy to serve the different customer segments, so you can avoid multiple product versions. Your product design will also need to accommodate customizations, that each customers may make within their instance of your product, without impacting their ability to receive product upgrades from you. |
| ☐ | 7.3.17 How will you manage configuration within your application? | Most of your customers will want to make changes to the product, based on the needs of their organization. The way your product is 'packaged' will determine what kind of changes your customers may make, without losing their ability to receive upgrades from you. You will also need to determine how to convince your customers to pay you (or another systems integrator) for the changes that they may need for their environment (typically, customers don't like paying for services in the cloud model). |

| ☒ | Question | Why this matters |
|---|----------|------------------|
| ☐ | 7.3.18  Are you considering using Agile methodologies? | Agile methodologies, such as Scrum, have been discussed a lot in the Cloud world. They require less planning and documentation and can be loosely structured. However, since so many critical factors will drive your product design before you *lock down* the contents of your package, Agile may significantly increase your deployment and upgrade costs. You will be better off sticking to the waterfall paradigm, getting all of your requirements and architecture straightened out before you develop. The alternative will be to sacrifice multi-tenancy, which is far more important than any development methodology. |
| ☐ | 7.3.19  You follow Agile today. Can you use it anytime with Force.com? | Maybe, after you go through the first couple of versions of your product successfully. Fundamentally, if your object model is changing with every release of your product, upgrading your customers to a new release will become very expensive. Therefore, you are better off creating a stable object model before adopting a more ad hoc development process. It will take at least two release cycles before you get to that point. |
| ☐ | 7.3.20  How will you handle regression testing for each release? | Since the Cloud platforms are relatively new, there are currently no automated testing tools available that can support regression testing for a Force.com app. However, this may change soon. |

| ☒ | Question | Why this matters |
|---|----------|------------------|
| ☐ | 7.3.21 Can you use a version control system for development? | Source code control will be critical. The Force.com IDE discussed earlier is built on the open-source Eclipse platform, and supports the most popular source code control systems. Subversion is the one that is most commonly used. |

## 7.4 Deploying your product

Writing your application in the Cloud opens up a new world of possibilities to make it available to a worldwide audience. This sounds great in theory but it also leads to a series of new challenges. Deploying and supporting customers remotely, in partnership with other providers, isn't easy. It's even harder when your customers don't pay you a lot of money for doing it.

It's also vitally important, once your application is in the field, that you monitor its performance, usage and other metrics. After all, you will need to maintain a continuous relationship with your customers.

The following questions should help you think through some critical items that need to be taken care of, after your app is developed.

| ☒ | Question | Why this matters |
|---|----------|------------------|
| ☐ | 7.4.1 How will implementation of the application to individual customers be managed? | You will need to think through how your app will be deployed for each customer. Most of these activities will be expected to be a part of your product installation, without an extra price tag. Will these activities be remote or on-site? What kind of handholding will your customers need? How frequently will your customers need upgrades? Can you force all of them to upgrade at the same time or do you need flexibility? |
| ☐ | 7.4.2 Have you created a customer on-boarding process? | Once a contract is signed, your prospect becomes your customer and the salesperson typically moves on to the next sale. Someone now needs to take charge of all the communication and steps required to get them up and running. You also need to make sure that their very first experience dealing with your company is a positive one and you start your new relationship on the right foot. Have you thought through that process to make sure you create a seamless customer on-boarding experience? |
| ☐ | 7.4.3 Can you provide professional services support to a global customer base? | If your application is going to be deployed to a global audience (which can easily happen in the Cloud world) you need to think beyond just the technical issues. You may need professional services as part of your solution and you need to consider how you will manage this on a global basis. These services may include requirements gathering, customizations and data migration. You may also have to think about working with other salesforce.com consulting partners to augment your professional services team. |

| ☒ | Question | Why this matters |
|---|----------|------------------|
| ☐ | 7.4.4 How will training be performed? | Training may or may not be a paid activity, depending on your app and the expectations. Since your ultimate goal will be to retain your customers so they renew your contracts year after year, it will be in your interest to ensure that all users are not just trained but are completely hooked on your app. This may require you to invest in a strong training capability. Your business teams will need to figure out how to fund this activity and whether customers can be charged for it. |
| ☐ | 7.4.5 Will your customers be able to integrate directly to their internal or other third-party systems? | Yes. Force.com provides a robust web services API that can facilitate this. In addition there are several third-party vendors such as *Informatica*, *Pervasive* and *Cast Iron* that provide integration middleware (already integrated on the Salesforce side) that can offer other additional features like error handling that may be critical for some of your customers. You will need to package your app appropriately, to take advantage of the various integration options available for your customers. |
| ☐ | 7.4.6 How will you manage support and help desks? | Will your application be supported during working hours within your country, follow-the-sun, or 24 hours? Will you have lower cost support channels such as email and chat? Will you charge for the support? |

| ☒ | Question | Why this matters |
|---|----------|------------------|
| ☐ | 7.4.7 What online training tools and self service support are provided? | The typically low revenue per user in the Cloud model means that you cannot afford to have the user contacting you on a regular basis. To reduce the need for customers to call the helpdesk and to increase the use of a service, you will normally provide online tools. How are these incorporated into the service? |
| ☐ | 7.4.8 What level of monitoring will you need within your application? | In an on-premise model, it becomes critical to monitor how the application is performing. You need to keep an eye on CPU utilization, memory allocation and hundreds of other variables, for a customer installation. However, a big advantage of a multi-tenant Cloud infrastructure like Force.com is that you will not need to monitor most of these, if your app is built natively (for composite apps, you may need to figure this out, though). Load balancing and scalability will not be your headaches – you'd be paying salesforce.com to deal with all of that. |
| ☐ | 7.4.9 Will customers require dedicated disaster recovery solutions? | There is no disaster recovery required for Force.com. By definition, the use of Cloud Computing negates the need for this – salesforce.com is responsible for disaster recovery through their network of datacenters around the world. A common theme with Force.com is simplicity at the cost of control. |

# Chapter 8

# Results not theory

*To acquire knowledge, one must study; but to acquire wisdom, one must observe.*

**Marilyn vos Savant (author, lecturer, playwright and listed in Guinness Book of Records under "Highest IQ")**

CLOUD Computing sounds great in theory. The last Chapters of questions were valuable – but not very exciting or engaging[12]. They could hardly be described as fun. What the book is missing are some case studies which bring the Smart Questions to life.

Now life isn't always fun. Some of the stories are painful and expensive. But that makes them all the more valuable.

If we'd interspersed these stories with the questions it would have made the last Chapters too long. It would also have prevented you using the questions as checklists or aide-memoires. So we've grouped together our list of stories in this Chapter. I'm sure that you have your own stories – both positive and negative - so let us know them:

*stories@Smart-Questions.com*

*amisra@navatargroup.com*

*ian.gotts@nimbuspartners.com*

---

[12] I struggle to think any activity which is BOTH valuable and really fun – apart from setting up and running companies.

---

# Case study: CVM Solutions

*Our early work with Navatar helped us see Force.com's potential to help us innovate at a rapid pace.*

**Rajesh Voddiraju, President, CVM Solutions**    *www.cvmsolutions.com*

 ## Clear skies - life was fine before the Cloud

CVM Solutions is one of the fastest growing providers of supplier management solutions as well as a Cloud-computing pioneer. For the past 7 years, the company has been helping Fortune 500 clients centralize vendor management, manage supplier diversity, and mitigate risk using products built on its proprietary platform. To sustain growth and ensure the scalability and innovation its customers demand the company had been looking for new ideas and solutions.

 ## Clouds forming – drivers to migrate

Rajesh Voddiraju, CVM's president, is a former IT consultant with a background in CRM and a long-time believer in Cloud Computing. When the company started in 2002, Voddiraju and the other founders knew that offering a Cloud-based solution was essential to position their fledgling company for long-term growth. For its first Cloud-computing applications, CVM developed a proprietary platform, built on Microsoft technologies, including SQL server, the .NET framework, and C#.

When Voddiraju and team kicked off planning for Supplier Central version 10.0, they considered alternatives to their proprietary platform for the first time. "A lot of our clients were looking to expand their footprint, so scalability was becoming more important," he explains. "Last year, we processed more than 16 million individual suppliers. We need to ensure that as we take on more clients, we can continue to deliver the performance they demand."

"Over time, we also found that we needed a way to deliver customer-driven innovation faster, better, and in a more cost effective manner," he continues. "We're self-funded, so we're even more particular about how we spend our dollars. Solving our clients' business issues is the most important thing."

After a proof of concept with Navatar Group, CVM decided to port its Supplier Central™ products to Force.com.

 ## Cloud cover – the Cloud solution

More than half of CVM's clients use salesforce.com to help run their businesses. The automatic integration of Supplier Central v. 10 and Salesforce CRM is powerful, and Voddiraju plans to connect the two even more tightly in the future. He says, "For the first time, customers will be able to link suppliers directly to customer revenue. Measuring trade issues and supplier risk impact are increasingly important in today's global economy, and we'll make it easier than ever before for our customers to see the effect."

CVM has already released the new version of Supplier Central with several leading Fortune 500 clients. Following the rollout, the company plans to make its applications available on the AppExchange, so salesforce.com customers can easily find and test drive them. Voddiraju sees the AppExchange as a key vehicle for reaching potential customers. "As more and more IT organizations adopt Force.com, they'll be an increasing influencer for our products, and we want to ensure that we're top of mind for these tech users."

The salesforce.com name is a key selling point for the new version. "We primarily serve blue chip, Fortune 1,000 companies like AT&T, Dell, and Wal-Mart. One of the big things for them is making sure that they're selecting a vendor or supplier that's going to be around for a long time. Salesforce.com gives them that security," he adds. "We're looking forward to working together for a long time."

# Case study: FinancialForce.com

*We have been impressed by what FinancialForce.com has achieved in such a short space of time.*

**Jason Cremins, CEO, Remote Media**        *www.FinancialForce.com*

FinancialForce.com was formed in 2009 by the Dutch group UNIT4 (and its UK-headquartered finance and accounting software operation, CODA), with a minority interest being held by salesforce.com. Originally conceived by CODA as CODA 2go, the FinancialForce.com application is 100% native on the Force.com platform and is built as fully integrated with the salesforce.com Sales and Service Clouds.

 ## Clear skies - life was fine before the Cloud

The CODA team are experts in on-premise finance and accounting applications, with over 30 years of experience and customers operating across more than 100 countries. CODA financial accounting software has a formidable reputation, and resides on local servers in some 2,600 mid-to-large organizations around the world.

"We have a 'multi-everything' approach: multi-lingual, multi-currency, multi-company. In the accounting world, we enjoy enormous credibility, especially among mid- to enterprise-level organizations," said David Turner, UNIT4 Group Marketing Director.

 ## Clouds forming - drivers to migrate

"On-demand solutions are not only growing in popularity, but – as salesforce.com has proven – can have broad market penetration," said Jeremy Roche, CEO of FinancialForce.com and Member of the UNIT4 Managing Board. "It became clear to us that we needed to be on an on-demand platform, and that ultimately meant building on Force.com."

"Moving to the Cloud was a logical extension of the CODA team's 'open platform' strategy. Creating FinancialForce.com with salesforce.com created a new vehicle to take our Force.com products to market and allowed us to invest in building dedicated development, marketing, sales, consulting and support teams specifically aimed at delivering world-class accounting solutions on the Force.com platform. Delivering FinancialForce Accounting on the Force.com platform will allow us to offer our product portfolio to a far wider range of businesses," said Roche.

The CODA development team had been reviewing the emerging market for on-demand applications for some time, but the commitment to build on the Force.com platform came from a desire to concentrate on building the applications rather than trying to understand and manage the underlying infrastructure of a SaaS environment, coupled with the realization that accounting was a logical extension to the successful Sales and Service Clouds from salesforce.com.

##  Cloud cover – the Cloud solution

The FinancialForce.com service has DNA from the CODA product's award-winning 'multi-everything' finance functionality: adapted for organizations of all types and sizes; hosted as an on-demand service on salesforce.com's infrastructure. It is the only enterprise-level application to be designed, built and delivered Force.com.

FinancialForce Accounting debuted with sales invoicing and accounts receivable functionality, addressing a clear demand from many organizations for a seamless, software-as-a-service solution to manage the process of converting orders into cash and rapidly followed this with a full accounting solution, covering: general ledger, receivables, payables and any number of user defined ledgers. Winter 10 saw the addition of automation around debt control amongst other innovative features.

The innovation is far from over. At the time of writing, FinancialForce.com is due to deliver its Spring 10 release and is working on integration with Chatter from salesforce.com.

"We have planned a full roadmap based on our experience in the financials market" said Debbie Ashton, VP, Product. "In addition, we are aiming to build new and innovative applications based on salesforce.com's enhancements to the Force.com platform."

 **Sunny spells - the benefits**

When FinancialForce.com first set out to build an online accounting solution, the project at first seemed daunting. "We knew that developing our own on-demand platform in-house would be a lengthy and expensive project and that we were looking at least two years before we could start building the solution on the platform," says Ashton. "Using Force.com allowed us to start building application within weeks of making our decision to go ahead, wiping at least two years from our original project estimates".

"FinancialForce.com's on-demand accounting is simple to set up and use and cost-effective to run, and for many companies and subsidiaries, it will better meet their accounting requirements than on-premises software," said Jeremy Roche, CEO FinancialForce.com. "We expect it to quickly become the de facto Cloud accounting solution for salesforce.com customers, as well as those companies that are looking for an online accounting application that is more sophisticated than others on the market, without the complexity and cost that often implies."

# Case study: HandsOn Network

*Non-profits have the same needs that any user does - they want good, fast and cheap technology. Delivering software that meets those needs requires a creative approach to both development and the business model.*

HandsOn
NETWORK

**Andrew Drake, CTO, HandsOn Network**          *www.HandsOnNetwork.org*

 ## Clouds forming - drivers to migrate

HandsOn Network, the volunteer-focused arm of Points of Light Institute, is the largest volunteer network in the nation and includes 250 HandsOn Action Centers in 16 countries. HandsOn includes a powerful network of more than 70,000 corporate, faith and nonprofit organizations that are answering the call to serve and creating meaningful change in their communities. Annually, the network delivers approximately 30 million hours of volunteer service valued at $626 million.

The core technology products used by the 250 HandsOn Action Centers – a volunteer management system critical to the volunteer centers in their networks – were getting obsolete. They were increasingly difficult and expensive to support/enhance, and not interoperable. Points of Light explored other options to cope with high customer expectations despite limited internal technology capability and shrinking customer budgets. Salesforce.com and Force.com, widely adopted by non-profits and corporations, offered the potential to reduce the ongoing maintenance costs by 50%. It seemed the most viable alternative.

## Cloud cover – the Cloud solution

It took a new business and revenue model to rebuild the volunteer management application on the Force.com platform. In addition to the app, the idea was to create a data hub that would aggregate all volunteer opportunities from the various HandsOn centers. These volunteer opportunities would then be channeled to corporations using Salesforce CRM.

Points Of Light launched the project to develop HandsOn Connect with an eight month timetable. In addition they started working on the plan to build another version of HandsOn Connect that corporations would use and pay for, to get connected to local nonprofits and communities. To reduce the costs, they created a partnership with Navatar Group to help build, market and support the new Force.com service.

## Sunny spells - the benefits

HandsOn Connect was launched at the National Conference on Volunteering and Service in New York in June 2010. It is the first Cloud Computing solution to help nonprofits improve how they manage everything from volunteer recruitment, operations and activities, to event planning, website and donor and contact management. The response has been overwhelming. It is currently being rolled out to HandsOn Action Centers. Nonprofits of all sizes are looking to migrate to HandsOn Connect and Salesforce, to manage their volunteer activity. In addition, several large corporations are in discussions to roll out a corporate version of HandsOn Connect, to help their employees volunteer.

The new model will now help Points of Light connect the volunteers, nonprofits and corporations – all through salesforce.com's Cloud. It helps them generate revenue from newer sources –affiliates as well as large corporations. The connectivity that the Force.com Cloud provides also helps each of the affiliates generate new revenue sources within communities and corporations. In addition, the move to the Cloud is also expected to reduce the maintenance and support costs by at least 50%.

# Case study: Jobscience

*TalentCentral is unique in that it was designed directly in response to small-business need, but can be used in any sized company. It can be up and running in an afternoon, works seamlessly with current applications, and is totally customizable.*

**Ted Elliott, CEO, Jobscience**

*www.jobscience.com*

 ## Clouds forming - driver to develop

A longtime salesforce.com customer, Elliott was an early supporter of Cloud Computing, visualizing not only the benefits for his company's operations, but also how the company could adapt its business model to better meet its customers' needs via the Cloud.

Jobscience's first Force.com-based product came about almost by accident. The company was asked to create a version of its recruiting system for Hire Heroes, an initiative of the Health Careers Foundation. The organization specializes in career placement for servicemen that have been wounded or disabled.

Elliott quickly determined that the best and most efficient way to deliver a high-quality hiring system was to leverage the Cloud. Based on the enthusiastic response of the organization, Elliott decided that his company should pursue a new business opportunity developing applications based on the Force.com platform.

 ## Cloud cover – the Cloud solution

Jobscience started by building an on-demand application to automate all aspects of a company's recruiting process. They now offers a full suite of talent management products including TalentStaffing for finding and hiring the best recruits, TalentCentral for creating and managing a company's career portal, and TalentPlan for adapting staffing plans to fulfill a company's corporate mission.

They've just launched a first of its kind, cost-effective applicant tracking system for only $1/user/month. It combines any edition of Salesforce CRM with an Enterprise account of Google Apps to give staffing companies and HR departments strapped by today's economic conditions an affordable, functional tool that introduces them to Cloud Computing.

 ## Sunny spells - the benefits

Force.com offers all of the power of .NET and J2EE without the worries of building and maintaining the infrastructure needed to provide on-demand solutions based on those platforms. Jobscience doesn't need to invest in hardware and software to deliver its products, or in the manpower needed to maintain them. Elliott estimates that the company is saving at least $40-50,000 each month by outsourcing the infrastructure. "Not only is it cheaper," he points out, "It is also more reliable."

Another key advantage of working with Force.com is the ability to quickly iterate so products can be constantly improved. "When we started working with Force.com we couldn't believe the difference," says Elliott. "Working with other technologies it would have taken ten times the amount of resources and effort. Now we can build new features and products in days or weeks. We can do prototypes virtually overnight." New products and versions can be made available over the AppExchange, swiftly reaching an appreciative audience.

As the market penetration of Cloud Computing tools grows, the opportunities for Jobscience will continue to skyrocket. By basing its development efforts on the Force.com platform, the company can continue to stay ahead of the competition with faster dev cycles, lower infrastructure costs, and the ability to leverage salesforce.com's own development efforts.

For Jobscience, the future is anything but Cloudy.

# Case study: Navatar Group

*Without the Navatar solution, I would probably need a back-office staff of 15 people to do this.*

**Julian Koski, CEO, Transparent Value (Guggenheim Partners)**

 ## Clouds forming - drivers to migrate

The Navatar founders, Deloitte Consulting veterans, had years of experience delivering solutions to large Financial Services firms. Navatar was born in 2004, when the founders saw the potential in the Cloud and became early partners with salesforce.com. The Wall Street office was established to bring high quality CRM services to the SMB market. Navatar's consulting practice flourished in the next couple of years.

True Cloud Architecture arrived in 2007 with Force.com and salesforce.com commissioned Navatar as an OEM partner to build and market products for the Financial Sector. It provided Navatar the opportunity to build a recurring revenue stream – the opportunity to transition from a systems integrator to a Cloud ISV.

 ## Cloud cover – the Cloud solution

Developing the first Cloud products for Capital Markets and Private Equity proved relatively straightforward. However, the first few customers taught Navatar some important lessons about multi-tenancy, value proposition, customer expectations and the need for cost containment. It was becoming clear that a different strategy was needed.

The product suite expanded to include Mergers & Acquisitions, Hedge Funds and Mutual Funds, while Navatar began redefining the value proposition of the offerings. Managing the trade-offs related to multi-tenancy became one of the primary focus areas. To contain costs, the product sales, product management and product support teams were set up in Navatar's New Delhi (India) office.

The initial targets were the SMB firms in financial services, which had been used to dealing with on premise products. They reaffirmed Navatar's assumptions and started responding to a very different value proposition, pricing and service levels from the on premise vendors.

In the meantime, other ISVs looking for a Cloud play and struggling with similar issues, needed advice and help. As Navatar started helping them, a new practice to help ISVs build, launch, sell and support their products, was created.

 ## Sunny spells - the benefits

The initial focus was on the SMB market – however, after the first 100 customers, larger financial firms started noticing Navatar. Big names such as Jefferies & Co., Guggenheim Partners and Carlyle Group, usually reliant on their IT departments, started signing up for the Navatar service. In a short timeframe, Navatar has become the leading Cloud provider for financial firms such as Mutual Funds, Hedge Funds, Brokerage firms, Private Equity firms, Investment Banks and M&A Advisory firms. Their Cloud products, built on the Force.com platform, are replacing expensive on premise products from larger, established ISVs.

The Cloud has enabled the 50-person Navatar team, split between the US and India, to sign up eminent financial firms in other countries such as Germany, England, Switzerland, Israel, Canada, Australia, Brazil, and, believe it or not, Kazakhstan! Customers, geographies and partners have been rapidly adding depth and breadth to the product suite. In addition, the Navatar planning team has been working on Cloud products in various other areas in the financial sector.

A financial firm benefits since they can get going with an application completely customized to their needs, while paying as little as the price of a coffee per user every day! They don't have to pay for any implementation, systems integration, training, maintenance support, or upgrades – typically big expense items.

Navatar's ISV consulting practice has also been very busy helping several ISVs launch complex Cloud products. Some of them, such as HandsOn Network's Volunteer Management Cloud and CVM's Supply Chain Cloud promise to change the landscape within their industries.

## Case study: Nimbus

*The process mapping was an essential part of understanding what we have and what we need. It was easy to see where Force.com could play.*

**Lucy Mills, Business Excellence Manager**

*www.nimbuspartners.com*

### Clear skies - life was fine before the Cloud

Established in 1997, Nimbus has provided Control software and services for Business Process Management. Control enables organizations to discover, understand and measure end to end process, align responsibilities, consider and include controls and governance. Nimbus Control then goes one step further to enable organizations to publish content as an Intelligent Operations Manual in the Cloud and on mobile devices, to all users.

Nimbus Control is developed using Microsoft technologies and integrates into core business systems such as CRM, ERP, document management, BI and email.

The demand for Nimbus Control meant that it was growing rapidly internationally it was clear that a robust CRM solution was required. Nimbus is therefore no stranger to technology and is an early adopter so Salesforce was an option.

### Cloud cover – the Cloud solution

Nimbus implemented Salesforce in 2003 and used the basic CRM with some small customizations for 20 users in Sales, Customer Support and Administration. The remainder of business had little or no association with the tool. But in 2006 Nimbus saw growth of over 200%, with new and existing employees dispersed across the globe. Multiple spreadsheets had emerged and the Salesforce application was data heavy and unfit to scale.

Nimbus took immediate action. Using Nimbus Control the organizational end to end processes were mapped. According to Lucy Mills Business Excellence Manager "The processes mapping was an essential part of understanding what we have and what we need. To start developing in Force.com before the processes were mapped would be madness."

Within 3 year period Nimbus worked with operational departments to understand the business need. Today Nimbus has over 700 user processes, 75 objects, more than 100 workflows and 15 approval processes spanning all departments and locations. "This is far bigger than we could have imagined, but the more we build into Salesforce the more we connect normally silo'ed departments. One Nimbus, everyone working together" said Lucy Mills.

But then the question was "Can't we sell the applications we've built on Force.com?" The answer is "No." There is far more to taking a Force.com product to market than simply Packaging it. Secondly as the apps have virtually no Apex coding – a key development objective - the IP is not defensible.

Walking away from what seemed "easy money" was hard for Nimbus, a massively entrepreneurial company.

 **Sunny spells - the benefits**

- Nimbus is able to build custom applications applicable in line with the business need, without the increased cost of software.

- All development is managed by Business Excellence, ensuring that Salesforce remains a business user system, and removing the need for developers and IT support.

- Connecting Nimbus Control processes with transactions in Salesforce has reduced the training requirements by 50%

- By engaging the process first Nimbus is able to realize change quickly and help users to adapt with the support of Storyboard training guides in Nimbus Control

Nimbus has recognized the power of Force.com internally, but has stayed focused on selling Nimbus Control to support Salesforce implementations.

# Chapter 9

# The final word

*A conclusion is the place where you got tired of thinking.*

**Albert Bloch (American Artist, 1882 – 1961)**

W HEN talking to people about Force.com the normal first question is "I have this application, or I want to do this – should I use Force.com?"

With Force.com its applicability is as much to do with your company's goals and circumstances as the application or technology you want to build. Many of the questions are business related rather than technical.

This comes as a disappointment to many techies who "Just want to start learning, exploring and building". Thinking and then thinking some more is far harder than coding. But it is the best way of building a profitable sustainable business.

Beware - everyone at the moment is billing themselves as a Cloud. Cloud is the new buzz word for the Internet. Many people such as traditional hosting companies now claim to be the Cloud. You'll hear talk of public and private Clouds and every combination of everything under the sun. It's Cloud Computing, otherwise known as utility computing, which you need to seek out. There are far fewer vendors able to offer this.

The only way Cloud Computing will work for you, as a software vendor, is if you can make your product multi-tenant. That means not having 1000 different versions of your product floating around to serve each customer. If your product isn't multi-tenant, your costs of maintaining all the installations will drive you out of business soon. Multi-tenancy is a necessary, but not sufficient, condition for success. There are other extremely important questions to ask, such as:

**Business Model** - *Is the Cloud model the right model for you?* You may be very tempted to view this exercise as just another language or architecture to learn and expect that the cash registers will start ringing once your product is built and launched. In reality, Cloud is not about selling a 'product' – it is a mechanism to help you provide a 'service'. Business customers demand much higher service levels from a Cloud offering. Before jumping in, you must understand the most significant aspects to service delivery that you will be forced to deal with. They will help you decide if the model is right for you.

**Customers** – *Why will anyone buy your Cloud service?* Don't assume that you know your customers - the expectation from a Force-com based Cloud service will be very different from your On-Premise product.

    i.      your market segment may change.
    ii.     your customers will demand constant improvement.
    iii.    their expectations may also be related to features provided by salesforce.com.

It's very important to know what your customers would want from your new service, before you build it. Do not waste your time with "feel good" visual or technical prototypes. Invest in a Proof Of Concept designed to help pre-empt customer expectations and create a real product strategy.

**Financial Model** - *Will you make money on your Force.com service?* Here's an example of an ISV's expectation: they were hoping to sell 70,000 subscribers in 3 years after building their product on Force.com for $100k. Really? If that's the kind of math that your financial model stands on, think again. The costs of building, maintaining, implementing, supporting and upgrading all versions of your service will be much, much higher. You must factor in all the expense items. You also need a reality check on the number of subscriptions you will sell and the price/seat you will get. Otherwise, you will be losing money and hair.

**Partnership** - *Will salesforce.com help you sell your Cloud service?* Building a product on their platform implies significant dependency on salesforce.com. Ideally, if all the stars are aligned and if you catch the salesforce.com marketing wind, you'll have a ready launching pad. Conversely, salesforce.com's direct selling team may become your biggest competitor if your service is perceived to impinge on products sold by them. Start asking yourself some fundamental questions about strategic alignment, investment potential, marketing plan, sales alignment, existing vs. new salesforce.com customers and product roadmap as they relate to salesforce.com, since they will make or break your effort.

**Ability to change** - *How long have you been selling On-Premise products?* Sorry to break the news but the longer you've existed as a software vendor; the harder it will be to switch to the Cloud.

*Fact #1*: Every function of your organization will have to change significantly before you see any happy customers.

*Fact #2*: Your Marketing, Sales, Product and Support functions will all fiercely oppose the change.

*Fact #3*: Your On-Premise business will be running in parallel.

So, can you still change? Yes, but it won't be easy. Success will require you to turn each of your functional heads into key stakeholders of your Cloud service right from the beginning.

Finally, you will be reliant on the Cloud infrastructure platform for development and delivery. Choosing the right platform which will support you now, but also has the vision and roadmap which will support you into a murky and uncertain world of Cloud Computing in the future is clearly critical. It is the most difficult decision to make once you have addressed the business and commercial considerations.

Having considered all the questions you may come up with the answer *No*. That's a *No to Cloud Computing*, or *No to Force.com*, or *Not now but possibly later*. Any of these answers is fine.

In fact, *No* would have been a better answer for many of the organizations we have talked to who have launched, spent money, cannibalized their existing business and ending up with less than they started with.

What is important is that the decision has been made with due consideration.

And that is the purpose of this book

# Chapter 10

# Time to take action

*You can't cross the sea merely by standing and staring at the water.*

**Rabindranath Tagore (Nobel laureate, literature, 1861 – 1941)**

S O the talking is over. Clearly doing nothing and sticking your head in the sand is no longer an option[13]. You've taken the first step by reading this book. But now what should you do?

It's possible that the book has left you with more questions than answers – or you have skimmed through it and decided that it validates what you already know.

Not every question in this book needs to be answered. However, if the book provides you enough food for thought, to be able to start working on a business and financial plan for your Cloud business, you are on the right track.

You may still need help. The Cloud, being a very different business model, will force you to unlearn a lot of things your experience in the software world has taught you so far. That, really, is the hardest part.

There are a multitude of Cloud events that you can attend. They are good for getting the perspectives of multiple experts and vendors. Salesforce.com also organizes its own events that you may be able to benefit from. It is also good to talk to your peers that have succeeded in making a transition to the Cloud as well as those who have failed.

---

[13] The Cloud is here when even my 88 year old mother is raising it in conversation

After gathering some data, you may also commission a Cloud Workshop for your organization (Navatar Group and several others offer various types of workshops) to get a better understanding of the particular issues you will run into. The workshops may be more targeted and may actually help you take your idea to the next level.

And, of course, you can reach out to the authors with your questions or suggestions. We will be happy to hear from you.

# Notes pages

Notes pages

CPSIA information can be obtained at www.ICGtesting.com
224336LV00001B/54/P

9 781907 453069